MW01488150

LIFE
from
A
to
Z

Livia Spitz Steingart, Psy.D., M.B.A.

For information about this title or to order other books and/or electronic
media, contact the publisher:
Dr. Livia Enterprises
16601 North 40th Street, #204; Phoenix, Arizona 85032
602-923-8500

ISBN: 978-0-9910247-1-1

Printed in the United States of America

Cover and Interior design by: 1106 Design

Contents

About This Book

THIS BOOK WILL EMPOWER you to better yourself. We are each a work in progress.

Once I decided to write this book, I began by looking at hundreds of self-help books. Many were good. But there was very few that offered practical activities to effect change.

I wanted to write a book that you could employ in a useful way.

My goal was also to make this book fun, familiar and practical. With these concepts in mind, I based my book on the A, B, and C's. We are all familiar with the alphabet and it relates to a simpler time. Each letter has an article for a concept with a different theme. Following the article are activities that you may do to strengthen the idea in the article. You may read this book in order or pick and choose which idea (letter) you wish to think about and work on more.

I suggest that you begin with the first two sections. Articles A and B have core themes. A is for *Attitude*. You determine your attitude and it will set the stage for your life. B is for *Balance*. Each of us is composed of four parts, the physical, cognitive, spiritual and emotional, which need to be in balance for us to be whole. These two ideas run throughout the book.

Another re-occurring theme is a flower. We are also a product of nature. We start out as a bud and have to slowly open to the sunshine. The petals represent the different aspects of us. We too, get rained on but need that also to grow and bloom. Life is a process.

The title is my promise to you.

Life from A to Z; 20 Minutes a Day: A Guide to Creating a Better You.

ATTITUDE

A TTITUDE IS THE MOST CRITICAL FACTOR in determining how we live our lives. Attitude is the lens through which we see the world, and the lens can be tinted rosy, gray or in-between.

We don't see things as they truly are.

We see things as *we* are.

Perception is very individualized. Two people can look at the same situation and see two completely different events. For example, a child is repeatedly seeking the mother's attention. One mother might see her toddler's repeated attempts at getting her attention as annoying, while another might see the same situation as a blessing: She has a child who loves to engage her to learn, to speak, and to play. Attitude dictates the perception of reality.

Attitude is eighty percent of any situation. Environment and biology make up the remaining factors.

We control our attitude. Happiness is a choice. Feeling victimized is a choice. Doing nothing is a choice.

We have the power to choose our attitude, and therefore our feelings and our behaviors.

We have choices. We always have at least two choices: doing something or doing nothing. Yes, doing nothing is a choice that has consequences like any other option.

Do not underestimate your power. We do have the power to control attitude — and therefore, our lives.

Life is a process. Each of us is like a flower that starts out as a bud. Slowly, with nurturing, the flower blossoms petal by petal. This process takes time and focus. It is a lifetime process.

Storms happen, but it is that very rain that waters the flower. The sunshine will come out again. We may need to prune a little, and to provide nutrients. But we are meant to bloom, to open up. We are meant to be a beautiful flower.

Because the mind controls our feelings — and therefore our actions — attitude is the single most important factor in opening up and meeting your potential. Actions define who and what we are.

A positive attitude lets you feel that you can succeed. You must be patient with yourself — nobody is perfect, but you can strive to improve. As long as you keep going in one direction, you will arrive at your respective destinations — even if you have a few detours.

Also, once you realize that you are a work in progress, it is easier to accept yourself for who you are. If someone criticizes you, you won't feel defensive. If you criticize yourself, you won't feel helpless and hopeless because you know everyone has their faults. Everyone can do better, a little at a time. By seeing life as a process, you can more easily accept any setbacks. When you feel yourself stagnating, keep looking ahead. As in skiing, look forward at the trail, not at the trees lining the path.

When you catch yourself in a negative mood, ask yourself "why?". Switch your thinking to another track: Think about the positive aspects of your life. Walk away from negative thinking; avoid those who support negative views. Search out and stay with positive people.

Taking control of your life is a process. Like learning a new dance, you must practice. A strong positive mental attitude is built the same way physical strength is gained: by practice and repetition. Over the years you may have unknowingly developed a habit of negative thinking. You may believe this negativity is the way the world treats you, when in fact it is the way you expect to be treated.

Only you can change right now.

Realize that you choose what to perceive. You must make a conscious effort to change how you perceive any situation — and how you respond. As you become more positive and proactive, this way of thinking will start to become natural to you. You will see your attitude begin to blossom.

How you perceive your situation is critical. You cannot always change your world, but you can change how you see it. And it is this very attitude that will attract more and more positive things into your life.

A college student, Megan, had to get extra money for school. She took a part-time job selling shoes in a department store. The first week, Megan thought the job boring and dreaded going to work. But then she decided to make a choice about her attitude. Megan thought about what she could learn on the job. She started to notice how the manager handled problems. She studied the promotions and marketing for her store and considered whether or not they brought in customers. She thought about listening and trying to help her customers find what they wanted. Megan learned about the different types of footwear and which might be better in certain situations. She began to enjoy her job; not only her learning experience and personal growth, but what she could give to others. Her attitude had changed. Her "boring" job became a positive situation.

Life is truly what you make it. You can choose to look at a situation as a hopeless victim or as somebody who can learn and grow. You have the power.

- Would you like to change your life?
- Would you like to live the life you want but thought you could not achieve?

- Have you tried but failed to do the things you desire?
- Do you look around at others and feel they had a better break than you?
- Do you feel helpless in achieving your goals?
- Do you feel anxious at times?
- Do you feel depressed at times?

If you answered, "yes" to any of these questions, please read on.

This book can facilitate your progress into creating a better you. Try the activities, research for yourself, become mindful of your choices and appreciate your gifts.

Life is, after all, what you make it.

Make your dreams come true.

ATTITUDE

Activity 1: How to Improve Your Attitude Today

Below, describe a situation that you are not happy about and would like to change. Example: I have problems with my boss's tone.

_____

_____

_____

_____

_____

Write about why you are not happy about the situation. How do you feel in this situation. Example: I feel like she is rude and disrespectful.

_____

_____

_____

_____

_____

Think about this situation. Ask and research to try to discover the facts. What might have caused it? What may be the reasons behind it? (Remember there are always at least three sides to any situation — one person's opinion, the other person's opinion and the truth.)

Write your thoughts.

Example: My boss is too busy to stop and have small talk or explain things. Or maybe, she thinks I am so smart that she does not need to go into details since I already know. Or maybe, my boss believes it is unprofessional of her to talk too much. Or maybe, she has not considered her shortness to be rude and has no intention of hurting my feelings.

What can you do to make the situation better for you? Example: Ask questions directly to my boss so I can get more clarification and discussion. Or, I could ask her if she has any suggestions to improve my job performance. Or, I could just think that this is the way it is and it's okay.

Write some actions you may take in a productive way.

_____

_____

_____

_____

_____

_____

ATTITUDE
Activity 2: Self Improvements

Create a positive mental environment at home and at work for your attitude.

Try Post-It Living Reminders to better your attitude.

- Find an inspirational quote and post it.
- Put your goals for today on the bathroom mirror. ("I'm going to have a great day.")
- Post some positive qualities about yourself.
- Sing and listen to music when possible.

Before going to sleep think about the day's events to better your attitude.

- Think about what you did well. Give yourself credit for it.
- Think about a goal. Come up with a plan to do so.
- Forgive yourself for messing up and smile about doing better. Life is a process. If we learn from our mistakes, it is good.
- Think about what you have to be grateful for and/or say a prayer. Go to sleep believing tomorrow will be a good day.

- Balance your life throughout the day. For something that you feel bad about — equal that with something that you feel good about.

Put up some pleasant pictures to better your attitude.

- Add a snapshot of a person who inspires you or someone who cares about you, like a relative, teacher or friend.
- Surround yourself with enjoyable objects and memories.

Colors are also important for your attitude. Blues and greens can be calming. Look around your environment and do changes that make you feel happier.

Lighting makes a big difference. Poor lighting is depressing, so for the mere price of a light bulb you can make change your mood. The new bulbs today offer warmth or coolness to the light. Experiment with different colors.

Lack of sunlight in the winter can be depressing. Try a sun lamp to see if this improves your mood.

Clean up the clutter. I once read an article suggesting we can get rid of a third of our stuff. I did this and don't miss any of it. Go through your closets, drawers, books, and garage. You can put it in a consignment store, sell it on EBay, or give it to a charity that will put it to great use. Think of space in your environment as a commodity. Trade in that old pile of old magazines for pristine space.

Clean up the mess. Dirty dishes and dust everywhere are de-energizing. Put on some good music and get to work!

Music itself can be very powerful on mood. Find the songs that uplift you. I work in an office that has Satellite radio. The staff and customers like the variety and no commercials.

Open the windows for a better attitude. Fresh air and sunlight are wonderfully energizing. Get outside, even for a short break, and take a stroll.

Note how you place things in the room. Research Feng Shui. Place the more pleasant pictures or objects in clear and constant view.

Have comfortable furniture at home and at work. A good desk chair can make a big difference. A proper mattress and good sheets make sleep so much better.

Stretch for a better attitude. Bend backwards and forwards several times a day.

Concentrate on your breathing. Your stomach should push in and out with your breathing. Take deep breaths. Be mindful of your breathing throughout the day.

Be mindful that you have power. You can control and improve your attitude and therefore yourself!

BALANCE

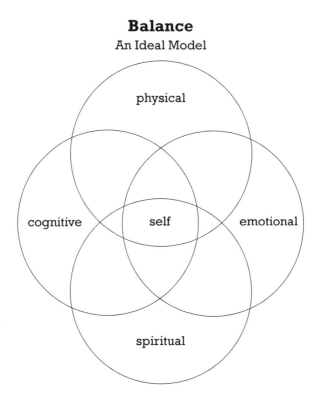

Balance
An Ideal Model

SINCE THE DAY YOU LEARNED to walk, balance has been crucial to your life.

13

There are four aspects of a person; spiritual, physical, cognitive and emotional. Each aspect plays an important role. It is important that all four aspects are in our lives with actions and thoughts. Too much emphasis on one or another part of you is not healthy. When we are out of balance, we trip and fall.

Spiritual

The spiritual aspect involves appreciating the order of the universe and being at one with nature. Spirituality need not necessarily be based in any religion. Feeling an integral part of something larger than oneself is the key and helps define each of us in relationship to the world we live in — giving us a sense of guidance and purpose.

Spirituality is also about the Golden Rule — treating others as you want to be treated. Each person should be treated with dignity and respect — defining "a higher order." This higher order gives rules for appropriate behaviors and consequences for ignoring them.

Spirituality gives us an opportunity to trust something outside ourselves — to help find our way, to solve our problems and to watch over us. It's a source of comfort and a connection to others. Spirituality facilitates healing, both physical and mental. (Read "R" "Relaxation Time" for more information.)

Physical

The physical aspect is the body. Your body is the container for you.

If you were given just one car for your entire life, you would take very good care of it. On this road of life, your body is your one and only vehicle.

Listen to your body. Be aware of aches and discomfort, and remedy them. So many of us put ourselves, our bodies, at the bottom of the list. We wait until something breaks and we are then forced to attend to it. Everyone knows the mantra of "watch what you eat, exercise regularly, and get enough sleep." Far too many of us ignore it. However, like the car, prevention is always less expensive and less painful.

A vast majority of us intend to live a healthier lifestyle tomorrow — just not today. To be in balance, we must make the healthy body a part of today. (Read sections "E" and "X"; "Eat Right" and "Exercise" for more information.)

Cognitive

The cognitive aspect is your brain.

Aristotle said, "That which is not used will wear away." Just as we must exercise muscles to keep them from atrophying, we must exercise our minds. Research is showing that using our brains maintains — even grows — brain cells. New cells are formed when you learn new things. And now research is proving that old brains can learn just as well as young ones.

Exercise your brain by reading, writing, doing puzzles, seeing new things, imagining new ideas, fixing things, doing art, sewing, etc. One purpose of challenges in our lives is to give the brain a workout.

The mind controls the body. (Read "Q" "Question and Learn" for more information.)

Emotional

The emotional aspect — our feelings — is also important to Balance. Emotions are the reactions we have to life's situations. We can choose our emotions, and we can control them. (Read "Y" "You Are In Control", "H" "Hot to Cool" and "W" "Worry No More" for more information.)

Nobody can "make you angry" or "make you happy." You actually choose to feel that way. Allowing yourself to stew over something just wears you down. You must recognize the reasons for the feelings, and then decide if you wish to accept the situation as it is or do something about it. Either way, you are in control.

Gaining control of your feelings about various situations can be achieved in many ways. You may gain more emotional control through self-therapy, professional therapy, and/or psychotropic medications (if indicated.) You may gain emotional strength by seeking knowledge on the subject, by reading or by talking with others.

The keys to emotional control are being mindful and practicing. It does get easier. Like playing a musical instrument or training for a sport, emotional control can be challenging at first. Start with the basics and gradually move up. Practice. You can strengthen your emotional aspect.

The following are two stories of people out of balance and the problems imbalance caused.

John was always using his emotional side to make decisions. He thought about how he felt about a situation and then acted. He did not research and think about things. John and his neighbor had been good friends for several years. However, one day his neighbor stated that John had put a fence on part of his property. John was very upset and called his neighbor rude names. John left trash on his neighbor's yard just to spite him. He lost a friend. A few months later while cleaning, John found the house diagram plans. He noted that he did indeed put up the fence in error. John would have done the right thing by investigating before acting.

Susan was a workaholic. Her favorite place was at the office, where she felt productive. She used only her cognitive side. In order to believe anything, she needed proof. Susan said that she was not a religious person. She was out of touch with her emotional and spiritual aspects. On a rainy day, her nine-year-old niece was killed in a car accident. Susan became depressed. She wasn't even sure why she felt so hopeless and helpless, being so out of touch with her emotional side. She had no idea what to do. Then, Susan began talking to friends about her sadness. She cried and laughed while talking about the memories of her niece. She found herself taking long walks and attending lectures about spirituality. Slowly the pain began to subside. Susan was comforted, and eventually able to accept the death. She also realized that there is more to life than just work.

Remember: Nobody ever said on their death bed that they should have spent more time in the office.

As you bring one aspect into balance, the other aspects align better. The four sides of an individual are like the petals of a flower. Having each petal open (and stay open) is a process that takes time and nurturing. But it is good when each petal is open and can feel the warmth of the sunshine.

Balance is the key to harmony in our lives.

Ask yourself the following questions:

- Do you spend too much time at work and not enough with loved ones?
- When was the last time you took a walk in nature?
- When have you tried to get facts about a decision before making it?
- Do you feel you *react* to situations rather than *act?* Reaction is more emotional than cognitive.
- Do you think about your body and how it looks more than you would like to?
- Do you spend more time and effort on your body than on developing your mind?
- Do you think so much that it paralyzes your actions? Analysis can lead to paralysis.
- Do you spend as much time or money on yourself as you do on others?

If you are concerned with at least two of your answers, do the activities that follow.

BALANCE

Activity 1: Mapping Out Your Balance Perspective

How do you spend your time?

- Log a week of your time in half hour increments. Write down what you are doing throughout the day.
- The total of your waking time is: _____
- Consider your daily activities. Identify the activities that were spent in each of the four aspects of Balance (spiritual, physical, cognitive and emotional). Add up the amount of time spent in each area:

The following are some examples of each aspect:

- Spiritual; walking in nature, going to services, reading from religious text
- Physical; exercising, playing a sport, using your body
- Cognitive; reading, listening to a lecture, having a discussion with others using facts, working a desk job
- Emotional; reacting, talking about how somebody treated you, remembering times of your life

19

Add up total of each of these four categories that you did:

Spiritual   _____

Physical   _____

Cognitive   _____

Emotional   _____

On the next page, draw your four aspects in circles (see Balance an Ideal Model, Diagram on Page 13):

Spiritual, Physical, Cognitive, Emotional

Indicate the amount of time you spend in each area by the size of the circle you draw. For example, if you spend the least amount of time in physical pursuits, make this the smallest circle.

Here is an example:

Total week hours awake = 112

Spiritual: 8

Physical: 14

Cognitive: 52

Emotional: 38

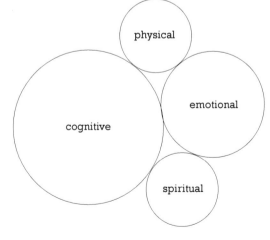

Draw your four aspects of balance below

BALANCE
Activity 2: Improving your Balance

Look at the circles you drew. Where are you doing well? Where could you improve?

What is your strongest side?

1. Write down what you are doing well. List at least three activities that you are doing to feel strong about this aspect or reasons for feeling strong about this aspect.

2. List at least three ways in which you could improve this side.

23

List your next strongest side.

    1. Write down what you are doing well.

    2. List at least three ways in which you could improve this side.

List your third strongest side.

    1. Write down what you are doing well.

    2. List at least three ways in which you could improve this side.

List your weakest side.

    1. Write down what you are doing well.

    2. List at least three ways in which you could improve this side.

CONNECTING CIRCLES
OF RELATIONSHIPS

RELATIONSHIPS ARE PART of what defines us. Community is more than those around us. It is how we relate to them and where we fit among them. It is our setting.

We develop in many ways. Regarding relationships, the process has been illustrated by what I call, The Connecting Circles of Relationships. The diagram on page 30 shows an ongoing process. Hopefully, we grow and mature, expanding into other levels of relationships. We need to reach out to others and have them reach out to us. This is a slow process that builds from one level to the next. Also, Connecting Circles of Relationships need to be nurtured and maintained once we have achieved all levels. Like a blossoming flower, the circles need to be watered and fed and do best when open and in the sunshine to take in the warm rays of others.

The process of maturing as described in the Connecting Circles of Relationships starts with the first level: the Self. This first level changes throughout our lives, as we explore and discover exactly who

Development of Connecting Circles of Relationships

———————————— The Supreme Being

———————————— Community

———————————— Friends

———————————— Family

———————————— Dyad

———————————— Self

we are. As we grow, we need to look outside of ourselves in order to achieve contentment and fulfillment.

As infants, we demand that someone attends us. We scream, we cry. This is necessary; at that young age we are helpless. We cannot even eat without someone feeding us.

Each of us then develops a one-on-one relationship or dyad, usually starting as caregiver and child and later in life becoming the one-on-one adult relationship. The next level — Family — broadens the scope, perhaps sharing your life with a larger family and/or maybe a few close friends.

The next phase of Connecting Circles of Relationship is to belong to a community at large where we share, give and take as needed. We feel part of something bigger than ourselves. It is important to have a nurturing extension that leads to community circles and eventually the world. Team sports, school events and clubs all foster this sense of community by bringing together groups with similar goals. We discover universal human traits, pains, needs and joys, and we learn new ways to think, to view the world. We discover we are not alone. We give back more than we take.

The last level of Connecting Circles of Relationships deals with spirituality — connecting with a force bigger than ourselves. The Spiritual connection is larger than the physical world we see. We may differ widely on exactly what this is, but it is imperative for us to feel this connection because the Spiritual aspect helps us keep life in perspective. We are only a part of this world (and a small part at that). Also, when bad things happen or we need something to fall back on, this spiritual aspect is beneficial. The thought that there is something bigger than us can be calming.

This growth through the Connecting Circles of Relationships is gradual and only works if we are open and willing to challenge ourselves. We grow from taking risks. Yes, mistakes will occur. However, if we never make mistakes we are not doing anything. Learn from mistakes and move forward. Nurture the changes and be mindful. Out of conflict comes growth.

Ultimately the Connecting Circles of Relationships looks like a full blooming flower. This diagram is below. In the center is you — the Self. The petals of the flower have opened and remain open. Each petal is a part of a social connection. The dyad is your significant other, like a spouse or dearest friend. The family/friend is your relationship with kin and associates. The community is comprised of your friends at all levels. There is a petal for the spiritual aspect, as well. Each petal touches the other and they all touch you at the same time. This flower is you. It needs to be nurtured.

In the diagram, the levels encompass one into the other, showing how one builds on the next. It is a developmental process. But these lines can and should be transversed. It is when we can go back and forth in the circles with ease, freely giving and taking, that we achieve the highest order of self-fulfillment. The more connections with other people, the more likely an individual will remain well. The reason is simple: The more social connections, the more support. This is like a bicycle wheel; more spokes equals more strength. It is important to connect at many levels with other people.

Connecting Circles of Relationships in Maturity

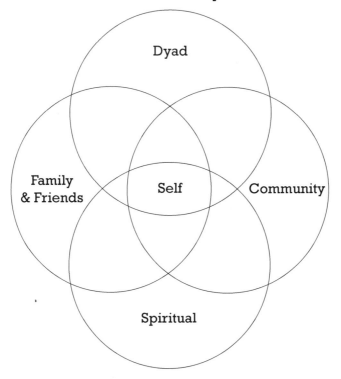

This diagram is you in the center with family & friends, dyad, spiritual, and community supporting you like the petals of a blooming flower.

It is a lifelong process. For proper balance in life, we must make the effort to be social. Staying in touch with friends and family are essential to being and staying involved with others.

Think about each question below for an assessement of your level of having relationships.

- Do you spend as much money, time, etc. on others as you do on yourself?

- Do you spend most of your time by yourself?

- Do you reach out to others?
- Do you stop and think about how much influence you may have on others?
- Do you think about how much others have done for you?
- Do you try and give back to the community by volunteering or helping others one on one?
- Do you feel part of a family?
- Do you feel part of a community?
- Do you think that others care about you?

If you answered "no" to any of these questions, try the following activities.

CONNECTING CIRCLES of RELATIONSHIPS

Activity 1: Socialization

List people in your life who say or show you that they like you:

1. _____

2. _____

3. _____

Write what each person does to say or show that they like you:

1. _____

2. _____

3. _____

Write activities that you do well:

1. _____

2. _____

3. _____

4. _____

5. _____

What people do you know who share interest in each of your activities? If no one shares interest in an activity, how can you meet people who do have similar interests?

1. _____

2. _____

3. _____

What you are working on to improve your relationships?

1. _____

2. _____

3. _____

4. _____

5. _____

The following section is to help you think about what you say or do to show others that you like them.

Often in relationships there is reciprocation. So, if you let others know you care, they are more likely to care about you.

1. Who are the people that you like?

2. How do you show each person that you like him or her?

3. What can you do better to show appreciation to others?

CONNECTING CIRCLES of RELATIONSHIPS

Activity 2: Having contact with people is important. We are social beings.

This activity is best done in sequence.

- Step 1. Contact a friend or family member that you can support and be supported by.

- Step 2. Ask how he or she is and LISTEN! Listening is important to making people feel connected to you. (See section "L" on "Listen" for further information.)

- Step 3. Set a time and place to meet and do an activity together.

- Step 4. (optional) Draw a picture of you and your person doing the activity. Visualize the enjoyment and fun.

- Step 5. List five questions that are open-ended and may be used as conversation starters.

    1. _____

    2. _____

3. _____

4. _____

5. _____

Example: What is your favorite movie? Why?

_____

_____

_____

_____

_____

– Step 6. Think about how your social event went.

   A. Did you enjoy? Why or Why not?

   B. What could you improve for your next encounter?

   C. What was your favorite thing about this meeting?

DECISION-MAKING

THE NEED FOR making choices — come up on a daily basis. We make decisions constantly. Sometimes we have problems that need solving but sometimes decisions are just picking options. It is valuable to have a good process for decision-making. Doing nothing, by the way, is a choice.

It is the way we handle problems — the choices we make — that determines our future.

Many people become frightened or overwhelmed about decisions and choices. Yet we can set up a system to solve problems. Teachers have always told us to do our homework. As an adult it is especially important.

It is necessary to do your research and evaluating.

Doing your research is about having the right facts and then being able to make the best decision possible. It's not about assuming that what other people say is correct. Seek good advisers, ask questions, listen, research, look at the past history, and do the math.

The emphasis is on thinking for yourself and considering the consequences of your decisions and therefore, your actions.

Here is an example of a time when I did *not* do my research. When my daughter was in fourth grade, I agreed that she would get a tortoise if she earned straight "A's." She achieved her goal. She called pet shops all over the area and finally found one that had tortoises. We drove to the shop and found a terrarium full of cute little 2-inch baby tortoises. One tortoise — an African Spurred Tortoise — fit in her palm and we took it home. We put it in a little terrarium and watched it grow and grow and grow. Within a year it was the size of a dinner plate! Having just assumed anything in a pet shop would be a good pet, we never suspected that this pet was the second largest tortoise species in the world. The Galapagos tortoises are the largest. We tried to keep it outside, but it would bang itself on the back door to come in the house. This was not a good situation for the tortoise or for us. Regrettably, we agreed to give it to a tortoise sanctuary recommended by the city zoo. A kitten from the shelter replaced it. If we had done our homework we would have known that this type of tortoise needed special accommodations. We could have avoided a lot of inconvenience and a sad little girl.

Doing the homework might make a difference in many aspects of our lives, from selecting the foods we buy to choosing a mortgage.

It is important to learn from the past. George Santayana said, "Those that do not learn from history are doomed to repeat it." We can look at events and patterns and recognize if we have seen a similar situation before. What was the outcome? Do we want to repeat it? Remember one definition of crazy: To keep doing the same thing and expect a different result.

When faced with a problem, tackle it. Get the facts. Research many sources. Learn from the past. Do your homework. Weigh the options, and then choose what you think is best.

Recall the image of a blossoming flower. Just as a flower has many petals, you have many sides. One of these sides is the cognitive or thinking aspect. Other aspects are the emotional, physical and spiritual sides. The thinking side of you directly affects the other sides. Therefore, you must do your best to make the wisest decisions possible at any given moment. Don't be afraid to make a choice. It's far better to tackle the problem and move on then to leave it looming large before you out of fear. Take control. Make choices for yourself. Yes, you may make a mistake. But remember that given what you knew at the time you made the best choice possible. Now, you may have other information. Learn and move on.

- How do you know if you need to work on decision-making?
- Do you have trouble making decisions?
- Do you feel stuck?
- Do you feel you could be getting a better deal on items or services?
- Would you like to make changes in your life?

If you said, "yes" to any of these questions, then proceed with the next two activities.

DECISION-MAKING
Activity 1: Brainstorm on Situations You Would Like to Change

Write five things in your life that you would consider changing. These could be your phone service, relationship, car insurance, new loan, long-term health care insurance, job, etc.

1. _____

2. _____

3. _____

4. _____

5. _____

Now, take those items and move on to Activity 2.

DECISION-MAKING
Activity 2

The following is a process that I devised for decision making. If you go through each step this method will end with the best decision given what you know at the time.

Sort It Out: A Problem Solving Process

S — Stop. Recognize that a need for a choice or a change exists.

O — Options. Brainstorm about your options. This is the homework part. Discover as many options as you can. Talk to others and do research.

R — Review. Write down each option and evaluate it. Ask yourself, what will happen if I do this? What will happen if I do nothing? (Doing nothing is an option.) List Pros and Cons.

T — Try. Take the best possible choice or option and try it. At a later date, evaluate how this option is working for you.

A B C D **E** F G H I J K L M N O P Q R S T U V W X Y Z

Eat right

As mentioned before, you are given just one body. If you were given one car for life, you would likely take great care if it. Modern medicine may work miracles, but prevention is always better. The body is a machine and needs proper fuel. If fuel is not supplied, your body will suffer. People must eat to survive. The key to eating right is nutrition and moderation.

But, food is not just fuel: it has many symbols and emotions. We relate food to love, comfort, even security. We even use food as a weapon.

Food can be a comfort. Some of us eat more when we are depressed. This may relate subconsciously to the times when our mothers fed us and took care of us. We often long for that nurturing. A glass of milk and a cookie may remind you of being tucked in and story time. You may think of food that your mother gave you when you were sick, like soup or tea with honey.

Holidays and their traditional foods may have special meaning and feeling. Thanksgiving reminds us of gathered family and friends, or warm celebrations and shared love. There is something about turkey and cranberry and stuffing that reminds Americans of giving thanks.

On the other hand, if you don't get along with your family, turkey and all the fixings may be stressful.

Certain foods can have a calming effect. Carbohydrates produce serotonin, which is a chemical in our brains associated with well-being and feeling good. You may eat popcorn or a bag of chips just to feel good.

Losing weight can be associated with emotional issues. And unlike some problems such as alcoholism, a person can't eliminate eating all together. Just like everything in life, being the appropriate weight for your height is about balance and choices.

Your body weight is not about eating such things as fats or carbohydrates. It is about calories. If you take in fewer calories than used, you will lose weight. The excuse of not being able to exercise and therefore gaining weight is overrated. Lack of exercise is only a fraction of weight gain. Your weight is about portions or caloric intake.

Losing weight is actually quite simple. The body uses energy, measured in calories. If you consume more calories than can be used, then the body will store it as fat.

The formula below shows this concept.

$$\frac{\text{Intake in calories}}{\text{Calories Used}} = 1 \text{ or balance}$$

For example, if you eat a muffin that is 350 calories, you would have to run for thirty-five minutes or take a brisk walk or bike for seventy-five minutes to burn those calories. Think before eating; for example, you may eat one third of the muffin. Here is another example: If you eat one three-inch cookie, you must run three miles or walk for four hours just to burn the calories. It is better to not eat the cookie or eat a small part of it. You may gain the satisfaction of a sweet, but not have all those calories.

Review the food groups that you learned in school. You'll find both serving sizes and food categories. Note the serving size. A serving of pasta, oatmeal or rice, for example, is half a cup or about a handful. Measure this out and pour it onto a plate. This one serving —with no additions such as butter or olive oil — is 100 calories.

As a nation we've grown accustomed to seeing huge portions on huge plates, in restaurants, on television and in magazines. Even one "healthy" salad offered in some restaurants can consist of so much oil, mayonnaise or other ingredients that the actual calorie count can exceed your suggested daily caloric intake.

While exercise is not a cure for overeating, it is necessary to the body, especially as we get older. It's like taking the car out of the garage and giving it a good run. If left in the garage, parts that are not used will deteriorate. Continued exercise raises the metabolism, so that more calories are used. Exercise also helps muscle tone including the heart.

Do not diet. The word "die" is embedded in the word "diet".

Diet usually means depriving yourself. But if you deprive yourself you are usually resentful. Statistics show that over ninety percent of dieters will gain the weight back. Once the goal is reached, it is back to the old ways of eating.

So, the idea is to change the way you look at food. You can have a little of everything. Eating right is about portions. Use a book or the Internet to research the calories of various food items. Keep a log on a note card. By cutting out 500 calories a day, you can lose a pound a week. This rate of weight loss is considered reasonable and healthy. The average woman needs about 1,800 calories a day. As you get older often metabolism slows down, so you need even fewer calories.

If you want to look and feel different, you must change your lifestyle and habits.

Keeping up your physical aspect is part of staying in balance. Eating right is part of this physical aspect. Also, eating may directly and indirectly affect your cognitive and emotional side. Eating properly certainly has to do with decreased risks of heart disease and diabetes, and it affects the ability to be active. Stay in balance. Eat right.

A healthy flower needs proper care and attention. A flower needs adequate water, food and sunshine.

So, do you.

You need sunlight, water and good food in order to blossom.

There are many myths about food. For example, carbohydrates are bad. In reality, carbohydrates aren't bad — or even fattening. A half a cup of boiled potatoes is about 80 calories. A slice of bread is about 100 calories. And to function, your body needs carbohydrates in moderation. It is what we put on the bread or potato that can add up the calories. For example, one tablespoon of butter is 100 calories.

Another common misunderstanding is about cholesterol. The secret to what has cholesterol is actually very easy. Anything from an animal has cholesterol. If it did not come from an animal then it does not have cholesterol. Per ounce, salmon has as much cholesterol as red meat. Four ounces of steak has about 90 mg. of cholesterol and 4 oz. of salmon has about 80 mg. of cholesterol. One large egg has 240 mg. of cholesterol.

All of this information is very easy to find on the Internet or in books. Education and knowledge are critical for your well-being.

There are many testimonials about being overweight. One testimonial is from Joe. He was laid off from his job. He started having problems in his marriage. Joe began to eat and eat as a way to comfort himself. His weight drew close to 240 pounds. Joe went to the doctor and was told that he was diabetic. His energy level was low and he was having a lot of back pain. Then Joe went to an orthopedic surgeon about his back and was told that to help his back pain he must lose weight. The body is just not equipped to carry all that excess weight, which strains the muscles and joints. He tried pain medications but those made him more sluggish. So, Joe decided to lose the weight and see what would happen. He began to realize that his weight gain was not so much about what he was eating, but what was eating him inside. Joe sought counseling. He lost 80 pounds in a year. His back pain went away, as did his diabetes.

What you choose to eat affects your body, mind and spirit. Be conscious of your choices.

Here are some tips to eating right.

- Drink a glass of water before a meal. It will fill you up.
- Take smaller portions with no seconds.
- Eat a little chocolate kiss, if that is your desire.
- Do not starve yourself. Eat smaller meals or snacks of about 100 calories. Snacks with higher amounts of protein are great as protein makes you feel full.
- Try smaller plates.
- Drink a cup of tea.
- When you go out to eat, ask for a "to go" box before eating and put half of your meal away. This reduces that meal to half the price, to eat another time, also.
- Order a kid's meal.

Understand food and how it can help or harm you. Examine what foods you need daily and how much. Look at your eating habits and see if they fit into your calculated requirements.

The simple key is mindfulness and moderation.

- Would you like to be healthier?
- Would you like to have more energy?
- Would you enjoy wearing a smaller size?
- Would you like to take more control of your body?

If you answered "yes" to any of these questions, continue to do the activities.

EAT RIGHT
Activity 1: Food Journal

Part 1:

> In order to know where we are going, we need to know where we are. Keep a food journal for a two-week period.

Get a 3" x 5" spiral notebook. It is easy to keep in your purse or pocket. Alternatively, you may want to keep note cards or use your SmartPhone.

> Date at the top.

> Each time something enters your mouth (liquid or solid), write it in your journal. Write the amount you eat as well. Portions matter and tracking portions is critical.

> At the end of each day, add up the calories that you consumed. You can find information about the calorie count of food on the Internet or in a Smart Phone App or you can buy a book with a calorie counter.

There is a SmartPhone App that counts calories and subtracts your activities at the end of the day for you.

Part 2:

You've done your food journal for the week. You may be shocked, as I was, at all the calories eaten. Remember we said in the beginning of the book that in order to change you must be aware. Now you are aware of the calories you take in each day. The challenge going forward is to eat sensibly and watch your portions.

Many people diet and lose weight. But statistics report that ninety percent gain the lost weight back. The secret to keeping the pounds off is simple: You change your way of thinking about food. There is not a need to diet and deprive yourself. You can eat anything you want, in moderation and balance.

Week Two
Go back to keeping a food journal. Be mindful and reflect on where you can cut calories.

This time, think about and research what you are eating. All packaging in the US has nutritional information. Take note of the "serving size" as the company reports nutrition. It is crucial to accurately count your calories. Have in mind an appropriate daily amount, and monitor your intake.

If you keep a food journal for two weeks, you will begin to calculate the calories in your head. We basically eat the same 30 items, making it easier to predict what the calories are for what you consumed.

EAT RIGHT

Activity 2: Think about food and what it really means to you

This activity will help you be more aware of your eating and the emotions tied to food.

Write down your favorite food or meal.

_____

_____

_____

Why is this food your favorite? When did you first encounter your love for it?

_____

_____

_____

When do you tend to eat more than you think you should?

_____

_____

_____

How do sweets make you feel?

_____

_____

_____

Do sweets relate back to a time in your life?

_____

_____

_____

FRIENDS AND FAMILY

FRIENDS AND FAMILY are important to our mental well-being. We are social creatures. We are biologically programmed to live in communities. Originally, this may have been for safety. A person could not survive alone, looking for food and protecting himself against predators. Humans needed to work together to survive. We still do.

If we are not around other people, we tend to become depressed. In diagnostic psychology, one major criterion for predicting a positive prognosis is the social connectedness of the person. The more people who care about a person, the more likely he or she is to become well and stay well.

This is just as true physically. Studies have shown that people who are happy and in good relationships outlive those who are not in good relationships.

Imagine a flower with many petals. It is open and vibrant. Each petal is a connection to the center, the core of the flower. Think of each petal as a friend, a relative, a group, an organization with which you have a connection. Each petal gives light and reaches out. Without petals, the flower would not be able to give beauty and joy and reach out to others. Without petals, the flower would not be able to get nutrients and sunlight. Without the petals, the flower would wither and die. The flower is you.

Infants form an attachment to a consistent caregiver who is sensitive and responsive in social interaction with them. The quality of the social engagement is more important than the amount of time. If an individual lacked a good attachment experience at a young age, he or she may not relate well to others throughout life. Poor attachment is a deep core psychological issue that is difficult to overcome as an adult. Securely attached adults tend to have positive views of themselves, their partners, their relationships and life in general.

This attachment goes along with my theory of Connecting Circles of Relationships (see section "C"). One level builds on the other. And if you do not have a strong foundation, the structure is compromised. The flower needs to have a strong center in order to have healthy, blossoming petals.

Here is an example. Hank lived by himself. He was going to work and then home every night. Hank liked to play sports, but since his knees got bad he could not join sports teams. He lost touch with his friends and felt a diminished interest in daily activities. He had trouble sleeping at night. His evenings were spent in front of the computer playing video games and eating. Therefore, he gained weight. This caused Hank to feel worse about himself. Hank was depressed. One day Hank's neighbor asked him to try to find his dog. Hank found the dog wandering on the next block. He walked the dog home and felt the most content he had been in a while. It was then that Hank decided to volunteer at an animal rescue. There he made some good friends. He talked to his friends about weight gain. They decided to lose weight together and walk the dogs routinely. Hank had made friends, lost his weight and was content with his life again. This was all through reconnecting with other people.

Even today in modern society, we need other people. The need to socialize is the reason that technological communications like

Facebook, MySpace and Twitter are so popular. People want to feel connected to others.

But note, according to recent studies, face-to-face socializing makes us happier than reaching out to people online. That's why going to the movies or a sporting event is still so popular. Sharing the experience, the roar of the crowd, the camaraderie of cheering on the home team is just plain fun. It is a community effort!

When my mother had a stroke, I was the main caregiver. I also had two small children. I was the sandwich generation, caught in the middle of taking care of children on one side and a parent on the other. It was draining physically and emotionally. I was exhausted. Sometimes I would pull into my mother's driveway before going inside and shut my eyes for a few minutes to get a little rest. I began to mention to others about my predicament. Others opened up to me and gave me suggestions on how to cope. They suggested everything from stress reduction techniques to getting more nursing help through her insurance. Sharing with friends and family made a big difference.

The family unit is important. Sometimes family may be tiring and demanding, but it is valuable to make an effort and be in touch. Remember that these people usually have much in common with you. You are linked by history, beliefs and values.

As the years pass, I notice that the items connected to family and friends get a more prominent place in my home. Gifts and knick-knacks from trips get placed in the closet or given to charity unless somebody special is connected with them. Items become priceless when directly attached to friends and family.

This need to love and be loved can be seen in the way we cherish our pets. Americans spend over four billion dollars a year on our animals. I must confess, I am a contributor to this pet phenomenon. Pets are a treasure — but they are not a substitute for other people.

It is important to connect to others: friends, family, groups, volunteering, etc. You may need to work on your socializing skills if:

- You find yourself sitting alone most days or nights.
- You frequently feel lonely.
- You feel you prefer the company of animals over people.
- You choose to eat alone rather than eat with others.

Do the following activities to improve social skills.

FRIENDS AND FAMILY
Activity 1

Step 1:

Start by selecting one of these suggestions to do. You may come up with your own also.

Go for coffee with somebody.

Join a group. One of the easiest ways to become more social is to join a group. It could be a formal club, church, synagogue, or temple. You could join a social organization. Every community has these available.

Take a class (even one night a week). This is a good way to meet people and improve yourself. Classes are offered throughout the community, in colleges, universities, hospitals, and religious organizations.

Do a potluck at your home.

Find an event like a festival or art show.

Invite another to go with you to an activity.

Volunteer. You may offer yourself to do charity or civic good deeds. This is a great way to meet people and feel good about doing something worthwhile. (See Section V — Volunteer)

Join a gym. A gym or taking an exercise class is a way to meet others. Try to be consistent and go at the same time each day. You can strike up conversations and be doing something healthy at the same time.

Look up free lectures in your area and attend. Public libraries or schools often have events. This is another way to improve your knowledge base while being around other people.

Join an activity club. Choose an activity that you enjoy. There are many leagues and clubs for everything from bowling to book clubs.

Step 2:

What did you choose to do this week?

Did you enjoy this?

Would you do it again, if not then pick something else.

FRIENDS AND FAMILY
Activity 2: How to Make Friends

When deciding if you want to be someone's friend, what are some things that you look for in that person?

_____

_____

_____

_____

How do you start a conversation? Write some questions that are not answerable with "yes" or "no."

_____

_____

_____

_____

How do you keep a friend? List actions.

_____

_____

_____

_____

Consider: Why is it important to have friends and stay close with family or friends?

_____

_____

_____

_____

GOALS

SETTING GOALS is the first step towards achieving what we want in life. Goal setting is about making choices and taking action towards meeting those choices. Doing nothing is a choice that has consequences just like any other choice. Be proactive. Take control of your life. Set some goals for yourself.

Goals help you prioritize your time and focus your energy. People tend to spend more time on things that are important to them, instead of getting side tracked by meaningless activities. By prioritizing, you can feel more in control of your life.

Goals give a clearer vision of the future. Setting goals spurs your motivation, and urges you to dream even bigger. Motivation comes from a desire and a purpose; goals should provide both. If you find yourself not motivated, you've selected the wrong goals. Those goals may be something that society or a friend or family member thinks you should want — but you don't really want them. Find goals you do deeply desire.

Setting goals helps you to see new opportunities. As you explore possible paths to the goal, take actions toward it, and find yourself around others with similar goals, you grow and learn. Life becomes new and fresh and exciting.

Wilma Rudolph was born into a poor family in a shack in the backwoods of Tennessee. She was the twentieth of twenty-two children and was born premature and frail. When she was four years old, she developed scarlet fever and pneumonia that left her with a paralyzed left leg. She had to wear a leg iron and was told by doctors that she would never walk. Her mother believed differently. Her mother encouraged her to meet her goal of not only walking again but running. She could even be a winner at running if she worked at that goal. Wilma began to exercise her leg. At nine years old, she took off the leg brace forever and walked on her own. She then practiced more and developed a pattern of running. At age thirteen, she entered a race and came in last. But Wilma did not give up. She entered every race in high school and after a couple years she was winning every race she entered. She was told by experts that she would never walk, but Wilma went on to win two gold medals in the 1960 Olympic Games in Rome.

Think of getting in your car for a drive on a Sunday afternoon. If you wish to relax and explore, you might just drive aimlessly, going down any road that intrigues you. But if you want to get to someplace specific, you need to have a route to follow.

Goals facilitate your growth and help you reach your potential. They allow you to stretch toward something more than what you are today. There is a thought, "Aim for the moon. If you miss, you will still be with the stars."

What are your goals? What do you want to do with your life? To answer these questions, think about what you are doing when you lose track of time — this is what you love to do. While we cannot always do what we love to do all the time, I think we can find a compromise.

To really find your dream is to understand yourself, your own needs, strengths, and desires. To look in the mirror — and see not what you are told you should see, but what you actually are.

To really find your dream is to try things. This means going to activities or places that you think you might find interesting. Trying new things is good for work and recreation. This is analogous to trying on clothes. See if it fits. Walk around a little. Look in the mirror. Ask yourself and others if it looks okay. Is it comfortable or not? As styles change, so do our lives. Changes mean that we have to go shopping and go back to the dressing room and try on new things. Evaluation is useful in your wardrobe and life.

Choose goals that are achievable; otherwise you may become frustrated and stop. Let's say you want to lose weight. Telling yourself over and over that you want to lose fifty pounds may not help you. The amount is too large, too daunting. Set a weekly goal of one pound, however, and then track your progress. One pound is not so difficult to achieve, and once you see it, once you check off each little success, you'll be amazed how motivated you feel and how the accomplishments feed your success.

Achieving goals takes time. Goals can be a map or guide to move you from where you are now to where you want to be. It's the route to the beach, with stops along the way. Remember to enjoy the journey. Remember it takes baby steps to get somewhere. You did not run before you could walk.

Setting goals gives clarity for what you really want and makes you more conscious of your every-day choices. Goal setting helps gives clarity about your own desires, instead of falling in with everyone else's wishes.

To begin, put your goals in writing. Taking this step makes your goals more real. Decide on the goals that really matter to you. Then work backwards to define short-term steps — goals — to accomplish each long-term goal.

For example, let's say you decide you want to be a State Representative. Now define smaller steps, such as getting involved politically, meeting the local people in your party, and running for a local public office. If you never accomplish any of these smaller steps, it will be very difficult to reach the big goal.

And, by the way, it's perfectly acceptable to change your goals. You may discover that politics is not for you, or that you really love working behind the scenes. You would never have known this if you hadn't pursued your goal.

We are as a flower that needs to be nurtured in order to grow. It is a process. But if we have goals we can bloom and reach up for the sunshine and dance in the wind.

At times you may not meet your goal. Then what? Do not give up; keep reaching!

Do not panic! Do not fret!

Your life is not over yet.

As an orphan once said, "The sun will come up tomorrow."

Remember the following examples:

> Thomas Edison failed over a thousand times before he finally discovered a light bulb that worked properly. We are all grateful for his perseverance.

> Beethoven handled the violin awkwardly and liked playing his own compositions. His teacher called him undisciplined and hopeless.

> Walt Disney went bankrupt several times before he built Disneyland.

> Babe Ruth struck out 1,330 times. He also holds the record for home runs.

> Winston Churchill failed the sixth grade, yet he became one of the greatest leaders of the Twentieth Century.

> Albert Einstein did not speak until he was four years old. His teacher described him as "mentally slow, unsociable and adrift forever in his foolish dreams."

Ask yourself these questions:

1. Do you go day by day without any accomplishments?

2. Are you unhappy at your work or lacking employment?

3. Do you want to improve your weight and physical well-being?

4. Do you want to improve your personal relationships?

5. At the end of the day, do you feel unsatisfied?

Setting goals is the first step towards achieving what you want, towards accomplishment. Many of us have looked back at our lives thinking, "What did I do with myself?" and being saddened by time lost.

Time is one thing that we can never gain back. Today is what you are given.

The present is just that: a gift. So make the most of each day. Create goals and focus on the steps to reaching success.

GOALS
Activity 1: Making a Plan

What do you want to achieve in your life? These could be achievements that you accomplish within the next six months, the next year, or within the next ten years.

> Be realistic. Dream as big as you wish for your long-term goals, but make your next short-term goal something you can readily achieve soon. Your long-term goal might be "huge success as a film actress." Short-term goals of taking acting classes and trying out for a local charity play are great first steps.

Here's a checklist for setting your short and long-term goals:

> Be positive. State your goals in a positive way. For example, "I want to be within my suggested body mass index" is much better than "I do not want to be fat".

> Be specific. Set a precise goal, put in dates and amounts that you can measure. This will help you account for your progress or lack of progress.

Keep short-term goals small and achievable. This will make your success easier.

Think about the following areas:

Financial_____

Family_____

Career _____

Creative/Artistic _____

Physical_____

Attitude _____

Fun _____

Community Service_____

GOALS

Activity 2: Developing Your Map to Get to Your Goals

Taking the goals from Activity 1, let's move forward.

Choose one goal at a time. What are the steps you need to take to get there? If you aren't sure, then what is the first step to take? How can you begin? Perhaps do some research or talk to someone who has already achieved the goal or would have knowledge about it.

Remember, it's better to take a step in the wrong direction than to not move.

Plan for Goals

Write down the following:

1. State goal:
2. Evaluate your current situation:
   a. Strengths that you have to achieve the goal
   b. Weaknesses that you have to achieve this goal
   c. Benefits of achieving this goal
   d. Risks, once this goal is achieved
3. List possible actions in order to meet the goal.

    4. Prioritize actions
    5. Write down time frame for actions.
        a. Begin date
        b. Action
        c. Completed date
    6. Write date achieved and celebrate.

During this process of seeking to achieve your goals, post your goals near your desk or a place where you will view them regularly.

Tell other people about your goals. This makes the goals more real, and makes you more accountable for achieving them. People will ask how you are doing with your goals.

Enjoy your achievements. Recognize and celebrate your steps towards your goal.

Write down your success story so you can look back later and realize how far you have come.

HOT TO COOL
(Anger Management)

ANGER IS AN EMOTION. And like all emotions, it has its purpose. The key is to be in charge: you control the anger. It should never control you.

Generally, loosing anything is not good. So, "loosing your temper" is not productive.

Anger causes both psychological and physiological reactions. It triggers the "fight or flight response," meaning your body readies to either do battle or to run from a situation. Your breathing gets faster, your pulse increases, your blood pressure rises. You begin to sweat. Your pupils dilate and digestion shuts down. These are the physical conditions caused by stress and anxiety.

These physical reactions are intended for the short-term only, giving the immediate adrenaline boost necessary to survive. But a prolonged or frequent state puts too much wear on the body. Higher blood pressure means a bigger risk of heart attack or stroke. And studies now show that stress conditions also affect our memory and cause anxiety. Life expectancy is decreased, especially when the anger lasts for long periods of time.

On the flipside, anger can be a useful emotion. Anger may motivate us to do something about a situation. It tells us that something is wrong and that we need to respond. Anger often moves us to action. If we help a friend who is being bullied, write letters to the government to protest policies, or help a stranger who is being victimized, then we've created positive change. We feel good about our actions and so we should.

Anger is the catalyst for many political and social changes. The women's right to vote, the abolishment of slavery and even the American Revolution were all the results of anger. People had enough of a situation and could not live any more with the status quo.

A response to anger may also be to recognize and address a problem within ourselves. If you hate your job, you need to evaluate your choices. Either find a new job, work to change things in the workplace, or decide that you prefer to remain and collect the pay check for now. You have the power to choose. (See "G" "Goal Setting".)

However, doing nothing and letting the anger fester can be devastating. Unchecked, this feeling can cause permanent physical and emotional damage. And the damage done extends beyond the individual. Being around someone with uncontrolled anger issues — such as a spouse or a parent — can have harmful and permanent emotional consequences which can manifest as low self-esteem, substance abuse, or even acting out the same anger, in turn doing harm to others. Physical harm may come to people around uncontrolled angry individuals.

Lori had grown up with an alcoholic father and a mother who worked many hours just to pay the bills. Lori would go out with friends but would often end the relationships with a fight. She would find anything to argue about and sometimes it would get physical. By the time she was twenty-six, Lori found herself alone and depressed. At work, she would at times lose her temper. One day, she got angry at a coworker for interrupting her and screamed at her peer. A complaint was filed. Lori's boss said that she was going to fire her if she didn't get her anger under control. Lori went for therapy. It came out in the sessions that she was angry at her parents for not giving her the childhood she thought she deserved. But the therapist pointed out that at some point we can't blame others for our problems. This is called maturity. We need to take responsibility for our own actions and feelings. Lori got the message. She learned that nobody makes her angry, but that she allows herself to become angry. She changed her attitude and is doing very well. Lori has been able to keep her job and even make some good friends.

We all become angry at times. We can all lose our tempers. But we can also become angry and KEEP our tempers. Let this emotion signal a time to re-evaluate, to rethink, to choose. Control the anger — never give it the power to control you.

Anger is part of your emotional side. Stay in balance. Losing your temper means your emotional side is out of balance. Without balance, you can't withstand the storms and may eventually fall.

Do you have an anger problem? Ask yourself these questions:

These are questions for moderate anger issues.

1. Do you find yourself closing your mind to exploring facts?

2. Do your children or friends portray you as the screamer?

3. Do you say or do things in anger that you later regret?

The following are for severe anger problems.

4. Has anyone ever said that he/she is afraid of you?

5. Do your spouse and/or friends avoid conflict with you?

6. Has someone ever received a bruise as a result of your actions during an argument?

7. Have you ever broken anything during or immediately after an argument?

8. Have you ever surprised yourself by how angry you became and what you did?

9. Have you ever hurt yourself or somebody else?

10. Have you even been so "blind" with rage that you could not remember what you did during your anger episode?

If you answered "yes" to any of the questions numbered 4–10, you may have an anger management problem that requires professional attention.

The good news is that this problem can be solved if you truly want to change.

> NOBODY CAN MAKE YOU ANGRY.
> YOU HAVE THE CONTROL OVER YOUR EMOTIONS
> AND CAN DECIDE IF YOU CHOOSE TO BE ANGRY.

HOT TO COOL
Activity 1: Anger Management Technique

The next time an aggravating situation arises, try this process.

Think about what you are feeling and learn the body signs of your anger. For example, when you start feeling angry, your heart rate may go up, you may shake or tremble, your muscles may tense up, etc.

Stop yourself before it gets out of control.

Cool Down. Give yourself time to think before you act.

- Politely, walk way from the person/situation.

- Count from one to ten.

- Take six deep breaths.

- Wait ten minutes before acting on the situation.

- Think of a time and place that is peaceful to you.

HOT TO COOL

Activity 2: Understand and Take Control of Your Anger

A. List the situations that cause you to be angry and lose your temper. Use "I" statements. For example, "I get angry when … "

1. _____

2. _____

3. _____

4. _____

5. _____

B. Take each situation and think about why it makes you angry. Is it truly an important issue to you?

1. _____

2. _____

3. _____

4. _____

5. _____

C. Look at each situation and think of another behavior that may be more productive than losing your temper. Other ways that you may behave:

1. _____

2. _____

3. _____

4. _____

5. _____

D. Evaluate your solutions and try them.

IMAGINATION TO REALITY

POSITIVE THINKING is an art. It takes practice and discipline. What the mind expects to find, it finds. If we think positive thoughts, we will see positive things. Positive thinking is a mental discipline that uses positive words, thoughts and images to succeed and grow.

Imagining our dreams as real actually makes them more likely to come true. If we think we can do it — and stay centered in that belief — we will find more and more opportunities to achieve our goals.

Every action you take starts with a thought.

Your mind controls your body, and attitude sets your thoughts. If you do not think you can accomplish something, you won't. In truth, we cannot rise higher than our dreams.

Imagining our dreams as real helps our dreams to become that reality. It propels our actions and affects what we see in the world. Imagination makes our dreams possible.

Imagining our dreams as real is part of the balance. We use our cognitive abilities to project our emotional, physical and spiritual well-being.

In the 1980s, I knew a doctor that was successfully facilitating the treatment of cancer. He not only used chemotherapy or surgery. He used psychological imaging. This doctor had his patients play Packman, a video game. He told the cancer patients to imagine as they played the game, that the packmen were eating the cancer inside of them. This imagery therapy, along with the help of conventional medicine, puts patients in a positive state of mind.

It may seem that negative thoughts come more easily than positive ones, which I theorize is due to constantly being barraged with negativity. Watching the news means being bombarded with depressing stories. You can always find people who are angry and who talk negatively at work or in the community. In some cultures, saying positive statements is believed to bring bad luck.

So how do we change our thinking?

It comes down to having a purpose and being mindful of yourself — watching and controlling what you say and do.

When you awake in the morning, think about all the good things that you are going to do that day. Think positive thoughts and get yourself going on the right path. You can even write a list if you like of positive things in your life.

Read a good thought each morning. You can get these on Twitter, on a website, or buy a book of positive thoughts.

As you go about your day, interact with people in a mindful way. Respect other people. Smile and listen to others. Every person knows something you do not, so perhaps you may learn something new from the delivery man or the cashier. The way you treat and value others demonstrates to the Universe the way you want to be treated and valued.

Positive thinking and imagery run through all aspects of balance. Cognitively, positive thinking keeps us mindful. This mindfulness affects our emotions and how we control our feelings. Spirituality uses positive imagery and thinking by being positive about the Universe.

Pay attention to your attitude. Watch your words, your reactions, even your feelings. Respond with the best words.

Choose the best attitude, the best feeling. Each choice is another step on the path.

Use your day wisely. Your time is finite. You can never gain back yesterday. But you can remember what you did positively.

We learn from yesterday
and dream about improving tomorrow.
But today
is yesterday's tomorrow.
— Dr. Livia Spitz Steingart

Make the most of today. This day will never happen again in all of history. The place to imagine your dreams, to be in that positive attitude, is today.

If you have any dreams that have not materialized, work with the activities that follow.

IMAGINATION TO REALITY
Activity 1: Getting to Know Your Goals

Post it. Read it every morning.

1. Put your dreams up where you can see them daily.
2. When you find yourself changing what you want, no matter how small the change, change your posts.
3. Post notes about your positive qualities.

Keep a daily diary. You can keep it in a spiral notebook.

1. Write down what you did well.
2. Write what you need to improve.
3. Look at yesterday's ideas and rate your progress.
4. You may want to revise your dreams.

IMAGINATION TO REALITY
Activity 2: Make Your Dreams Become Real

There are four basic steps to imagining your dreams as real.

1. Awareness. Write down your thoughts and feeling four times throughout the day, for example, write something after you meet with somebody, watch the news or eat a meal, or at a set time each day.

2. Rational thinking. Evaluate the thoughts that you had written down in the first step. Are your feelings justified? Challenge your thinking; is it reasonable to think about the issues the way you did? How could you look at them differently?

3. Prepare positive words or phrases about yourself. Start with strong and emotional cues about yourself and the world around you. Use the first person.

4. Post these positive words and phrases where you can see them on a regular basis.

Practice, practice and practice. When you start feeling angry or worried or depressed, ask yourself: Is this rational? Could I look at the issue differently? Could I change this situation? If it is your job that is causing you grief, find another job. Look for a different way of relating to people.

Remember: They don't have to be wrong for you to be right.

There are two ways of helping you maintain that positive attitude. These physical actions will lead to psychological change.

> Smile. Your brain emits endomorphones (happy hormones) when you smile.

> Breathe deeply and slowly. This will reduce tension and help keep your brain full of oxygen and focused. Breathing helps to improve your focus on reaching your dreams. It is basically a quick meditation.

A B C D E F G H I **J** K L M N O P Q R S T U V W X Y Z

JOY IN THE PRESENT
Here and Now

THIS VERY MOMENT, the present, is the only thing under your control.

Time is a concept. We often think of time as having three parts: past, present, and future. But the past is only a collection of memories. The future is truly our projection of what that time may be like. We cannot live in the future. We can only experience the future when it becomes the present. The here and now is the only place we exist.

It's the present because it is a *gift*. Enjoy the present. Breathe slowly and take in the moment.

People who do live in the past (meaning they focus on it) tend to be depressed. They think about what could have or should have been done. Or they may keep remembering past glories and wishing they were there today. An example of this thinking is the statement, "They just don't make things like they used to." In addition to being annoying, this thinking is also somewhat delusional. Cars, appliances and many other things are actually built better today.

We all know people who wallow in the past. A lady came over to my house for dinner. She could only talk about her bitter divorce and how badly her husband had treated her and her daughters financially. After a couple hours of this ranting, I asked how long she had been divorced. She replied, "Eight years."

"Wow," I thought. "It is time to deal with this pain and move on."

It is not healthy to ruminate on the past. There comes a time to "let go."

The past exists so we can use past experiences to learn from our mistakes and grow. Learn from the past. Then let it go. The past has passed.

On the other hand, those individuals who constantly think about the future tend to be more anxious than those who do not fret about the future. They tend to think about all the scenarios that may take place if "this bad situation occurs...." If we worry about something in the future, we actually experience the negative situation twice: once while we are worrying about it and a second time if the situation occurs. It is wiser to plan and prepare for the future as best we can and then let things take their course. One test I do to minimize anxiety after preparation is to ask myself, "What is the worst thing that could happen?" If I can deal with that answer, I let it be.

Robert was a father and now a grandfather. As a young boy in the 1950s he saw his dad leave for work every morning and come home late at night. Robert followed his dad's example. He got married and worked very hard to provide money for his family. He was a salesman and travelled seventy percent of the time. Robert worried about the future and what horrors it might bring. So, he worked hard and saved. But now as he looks back, he realizes that he never went to school events; he never spent quality time with his children. Recently, Robert has called his adult children many times, wanting to get together with them. But they are always too busy. He had never taken the time to be in the present and enjoy his family and friends. Robert is now alone. He is paying the price of not being somewhat in the present with his family when he had the chance.

Of course there are times when we should think about and plan for the future. We may need to work and save money, or go to school to create what we want in the future. We need to learn from the past. But the present is where we exist.

We need to understand that happiness lives in the present. Unhappiness and anxiety dwell mostly in the past and the future. We are unhappy about something that happened in the past. We may dwell on regrets. Or we may worry about something that might happen in the future. When you bring your awareness into the here and now, all worries of the past and all imagined fears of the future fade away. You see the world around you and start to see life.

It is this awareness of the present where thoughtfulness and positive attitudes are nourished and grow.

Joy in the present keeps us in balance. It alleviates stress, while simultaneously allowing us to enjoy where we are. Being in the present is important for us spiritually by letting us relate to others and the world. Cognitively, being in the present gives us focus. Physically being in the present is good for playing and relating to our bodies.

Ask yourself these questions:

- Do you find yourself ruminating on the past?
- Do you keep thinking about regrets?
- Do you worry about what is going to happen in the future without taking any positive actions?
- Do you miss the pleasures of everyday life?

If yes, take time to "smell the roses." Live in the now.
Do the following activities to focus in the present.

JOY IN THE PRESENT
Activity 1: How to Be in the Present

To live in the present, you must figure out the most important thing to do now.

This is an exercise in prioritizing. It has three basic steps:

1. FOCUS

If I could only focus on one thing in my life, what would that be? What would the second item be? What would the third item be, and so on? List five major items.

1. _____

2. _____

3. _____

4. _____

5. _____

2. SETTING BOUNDARIES

Look at your priority list. Think about how you spend your time. Are you spending too much time on activities that are not important? Eliminate those unnecessary activities.

3. PRIVATE TIME

Give yourself time to spend on yourself. Take time to exercise, be with friends and family, read, relax and enjoy being.

JOY IN THE PRESENT

Activity 2: Run your life. Don't let your life run you!!

Activity 2A.

Without moving from where you are now, look around you. Listen. Let the environment "talk" to you. Listen to all the sounds around you. Do you hear an air conditioner or the hum of the lights? Are there birds nearby or water running? Do you hear people in conversation, or a baby crying? Do not make any judgments about the sounds. Just listen. If the phone rings or somebody is talking outside do not respond.

Now notice all the different shapes and colors. Note that there is very little black and white in the world. Rather colors abound in our surroundings. This is true literally and figuratively.

After a while you may feel peacefulness.

This exercise demonstrates that we do not always need to respond to everything around us. You are in control of what you react to and how you react. You do not have to respond to every phone call or other stimulus.

You can run your life, instead of allowing life to run you.

Activity 2B:

Living in the present is to be aware of what is happening to you right now. It is valuable to stop and listen. Think about what is going around you. Take some deep breaths.

> Breathe in and count to six, hold it and count to six, then let out the breath while counting to six.

Do this exercise twice a day or as needed to combat stress, anxiety or depression. This is an also a stress reduction technique. Physiologically, the body can't be stressed when breathing slows down. This exercise will help you to focus in the present.

- Living in the present means focusing on the here and now. Enjoy what is going on right now!

- Make the most of each moment. You can never gain back yesterday. You can't focus on the future.

- Set up an environment at work and at home with little or no distractions. You need to be able to focus.

- Turn off the television or the computer when not using it. These can be diversions.

- Answer the phone only when you want to. You should control who and when you converse.

- Do something each day and focus on the present. For example, take a walk and enjoy the surroundings, talk to another person, do yoga, etc.

- Create things with your hands. (See Section U). Creating helps you focus on the here and now and what you are doing.

- Meditate.

KIND WORDS

THINK before you speak.

Kind words means weighing carefully the words you choose to speak. Appreciate the power of words. Words can heal and words can wound. Love, hate, fear, excitement, friendship — every emotion you feel can be inspired by words. Words can lift you up or drag you down. Words may encourage or leave you feeling depressed.

Words are the paradigm that we use to think as well as speak. We use words to order our thoughts and structure our reasoning. Words are culture-specific. Certain Inuit dialects contain over twenty names for the thing called "snow." There are specific words for wet snow, slippery snow, etc. Snow is a key part of the Inuit's life and their language reflects this idea.

The first words a baby utters have an important role. Babies somehow understand early that words are powerful. As we grow, we take our words for granted, even though the words we speak affect the way we see the world.

Most languages have titles to use alongside a person's name, allowing the speaker to show respect with titles such as Dr. or Mrs. When we want to be more familiar and friendly, we use first names.

Many sales techniques insist on using first names no matter the power or position of the client. Using people's first names diffuses a little of their power. Do we feel more comfortable having a critical surgery performed by Doctor James Shaw, or by Jimmy?

Kind words means choosing the best words possible for yourself, your mindset, and for those around you. The impact can be small, or indeed very large.

Think about two doctors with equal medical skills. The first doctor tells a patient that she needs surgery, hands her a brochure and walks out of the room. Compare that scenario to the doctor who sits down with the patient and explains the problem using diagrams. He explains why the body is hurting and how the surgery might alleviate the pain. I am sure you agree that you would rather go to the second doctor. But basically, it is all about the words.

Words affect the way we think and therefore act. There is a powerful connection between the words we use and the result we achieve. Whenever an issue arises in my business, I tell myself and my staff, "We have a challenge." I never use the word problem — that word has such a negative connotation. The word "challenge" offers opportunities for success. We want challenges. We want to succeed.

In the office, we should also be aware of the way we speak about each other. Consider the phrase: "She works *with* me." It says that we work together, that we are a team. We need each other. Compare that to the phrase: "She works *for* me." The latter creates a hierarchy, putting her squarely beneath the person uttering the words. "With" connotates team and peer.

Even when you need to "criticize" someone to correct a behavior, use kind words. Try the sandwich method. Begin with a positive, something the person is doing well. Then explain the behavior that needs correcting, and finish with another positive. If you only criticize, people become defensive and tune you out.

Watch how you use words. When you let words out, you can never call them back. Words do not stop and return. One you have spoken a word, you have given it wings and it flies off on its own.

The words you choose to use have a profound effect on you and those around you.

Words are important for balance. Words lead to thoughts and feelings which leads to — actions. Actions may impact any of the four parts of balance: spiritual, emotional, physical and cognitive.

There are many examples of the power of words. In 1776, a man felt strongly that America needed to separate from England. Thomas Paine wrote *Common Sense* to express his ideas. His book was instantly popular. It was written in common language that everybody could understand. Before this book was written, a third of the people were Patriots, a third were Loyalists and a third were neutral. Thomas Paine's words convinced enough people to cause the revolution that created the United States of America.

Other examples are the famous speeches by Martin Luther King, Jr. that lead to peaceful changes in civil right. Or, Winston Churchill's words that held the Allies together and gave people the hope and courage to win World War II.

Ask yourself the following questions and determine if you have opportunities to grow with kind words.

- Are you encouraging or discouraging?
- Are you finding and taking opportunities to build up your children, your spouse, and your coworkers?
- Are you belittling your own family or friends with words of judgment?
- Do you use mostly words that are critical?
- Are the majority of the things you say negative?

- Are you listening to yourself to see if your words might be hurtful?

- Are you using negative words in your head (negative thoughts) to cut yourself down?

- Do people consider you critical or judgmental?

- Are you aiding the destruction of your self-esteem by using bad thoughts about yourself, your health, your weight, your financial situation?

If yes, to any of these questions, then do the activities on the following pages.

KIND WORDS
Activity 1: Evaluating Your Speech to Others

1. Think of a time when you were critical of somebody else.

What was the situation? _____

What did you say? _____

_____

_____

_____

2. How could you have used kinder words?

If you needed to correct a person's behavior, remember the sandwich method: First a kind word or thought, next the criticism, and then another kind or hopeful sentence.

_____

_____

_____

3. A. Think of another time someone was critical of you.

    B. What was the situation?

    C. What did their words make your feel?

_____

_____

_____

_____

_____

_____

_____

_____

_____

_____

_____

KIND WORDS
Activity 2: How Do You Talk to Yourself?

This activity focuses on words rather than sentences.

Think of a time when you called yourself a name or put yourself down. Write down the situation.

_____

_____

_____

_____

_____

What did you call yourself?

_____

_____

_____

_____

_____

What were you feeling in that situation?

_____

_____

_____

_____

_____

How did you feel after you called yourself the name?

_____

_____

_____

_____

_____

What would have been a better thing to say to yourself?

_____

_____

_____

_____

_____

You may repeat this process as often as you want.

Now, think about somebody else about whom you said something unkind or who you called a name. You might have said it out loud, or you might have said it under your breath.

What was the situation?_____

_____

_____

_____

_____

_____

What did you say?_____

_____

_____

_____

_____

_____

What you were feeling? _____

_____

_____

_____

_____

_____

How do you think the other person may have felt? _____

_____

_____

_____

_____

_____

What would have been a better thing to say? _____

_____

_____

_____

_____

_____

You may repeat this process.

LISTEN

HEARING IS A physical ability. Listening is a skill. Let's consider the difference between hearing and listening.

Hearing is a physical act of perceiving sound.

Listening allows you to make sense of what another person is saying. It is one of the most important skills you can have. How well you listen has a major impact on your life at work and at home.

Socially, listening is vital. People need others to listen to them in order to feel appreciated and valued. Listening is critical to building rapport, showing support and understanding others. It is the foundation for learning, solving problems, making friends and maintaining relationships.

The world we live in has five ways to communicate to us — the five senses. The more alert we are to the information coming through these channels, the better we can respond and act appropriately.

We're now in an "information age," where we recognize information as crucial to decision-making, to learning and growing. To responding to whatever life throws our way. Listening skills determine the amount and accuracy of the information we receive.

Think about this: You do not learn anything when your mouth is going.

Communication is connection to others. We need that connection to be content. Also, listening well to others enhances these experiences with others.

To become a better listener, practice the activities in this section — making a conscious effort to hear not just the words the other person says, but to understand the total message.

Active listening is an active process with three steps.

Hearing is the first step. Hearing shows recognition of the words. If somebody said, "The days are shorter in the winter," you could repeat what was said to show you heard.

The second step is deciphering the meaning. To show you understand, you might say, "You are telling me the hours of sunshine are less in December than in July."

The final step of active listening is processing. Processing is when you weigh the meaning with your own understanding. You may think, "Yes, I have seen the daylight hours are much longer in the summer months."

We must strive to keep a balance in our lives. Listening helps us keep this balance. By listening, we learn and grow, allowing us to maintain all four parts of balance; cognitive, spiritual, emotional and physical.

Susie lived to socialize. Whenever she was with others she talked and talked and talked. She had to be the center of attention. Susie noticed that she was receiving fewer and fewer invitations. Finally somebody said, "Susie, do you ever let anyone else talk?" She stopped and thought for a moment: "I guess not."

Susie decided to make some conscious changes. She began making an effort to listen. At the next party, she asked open-ended questions and listened for the answers. It was hard at first. She wanted to constantly talk. But slowly by listening more, she began to learn about others and felt closer than ever to her friends. Susie grew to realize that conversation, like life, is a give and take situation.

Humans are social beings. Go to any part of the world where people exist and you will find communication. One way we connect to others is through talking and listening. No matter where, no matter how remote, somehow a language was created. Seat two strangers together on an airplane and frequently they start to talk. Think about this: We give somebody "the silent treatment" as punishment.

In any relationship, communication is crucial. Communication involves speaking and listening. Lack of communication is one of the most common causes of failure in any relationship.

How can you improve your listening skills?

- Give your full attention to the person who is speaking. Don't let yourself be distracted by other things around you.

- Stay focused. It is easy to let your mind wander, especially if you are not interested in what the speaker is saying. Perhaps you might become interested if you pay attention.

- Listen for main ideas.

- Let the speaker finish before you are talking. In other words, do not interrupt.

- Don't try to anticipate what you are going to say next.

- Respect the speaker and his or her point of view.

- Give feedback.

- Repeat for clarification. "So, you're saying...."

- Ask questions. When you ask questions you must understand and process what the speaker is saying. The question actually takes the information a step further.

How do you know if you are a good listener?

- Do you think about the concepts you hear from others while they are speaking?
- Do you ask questions for clarification?
- Do you come away from conversations thinking about the others' ideas?

If you said "yes," you are on the right path. On the other hand:

- Do you do more talking than the other person(s)?
- Are you often waiting to jump in when the other person is speaking?
- Do you find it is boring, stupid, or a waste of your time when others talk?
- In a conversation, are you thinking only about your next statement?
- Are you thinking about your next statement rather than processing the others' ideas?

If your answer is "yes" to any of these, do the following activities.

LISTEN
Activity 1

Here are six exercises to become a more active listener.

Focus. This means to concentrate and make no emotional judgments. Emotions can get in the way of you being an objective listener. Really try to study the other person's words with an open mind. Remember: there is a big difference between hearing and listening. Do this with the next person that you talk to. Focus completely on that individual. Don't allow your mind to wander.

Take a notebook and write down all the discussions you have in a day. Write down the subject and the points raised. By writing all this information down for at least three or four discussions, you will see your level of listening.

Do not interrupt. Don't formulate your response; don't wait for a pause to leap in with your own point of view. The idea here is to pay attention to the speaker's words instead of readying your own. If you truly listen, you might very well learn something. We can learn from anyone.

Write down any questions you may have during a conversation so as not to interrupt the speaker.

Maintain eye contact. Active listening skills require that you use both ears and eyes to listen. Watch the other person's body language. Studies indicate that over seventy percent of what people communicate is through their body language. Making good eye contact also lets the other person feel confident that you are paying attention and are encouraging.

Sit or stand in a position where you can see the speaker and he or she can see you directly. Take note of the speaker's body language.

Give feedback. Good listening is active. Feedback includes nodding and acknowledging. This acknowledgement to the speaker is important. Words like "I understand," "Yes," "I had a similar experience," let the speaker know that you are listening. But do not steal the conversation.

Write down some feedback statements. Then, see how well you are using this technique.

Questions are important for active listening. Questions indicate that you are thinking about the other person's words and processing their meaning. Asking questions shows a high level of comprehension and make you look smart.

Ask questions that pertain to what the speaker is relating.

Clarify what the other person is saying. This can be as simple as "So, what you are saying is … is that right?" This can be especially useful in discussions with friends and family as we too often assume what the other person is saying or hearing. By asking for clarification, they know you are really listening and not just hearing.

Write down some good clarification statements. Keep notes of how well you are using them.

Practice these skills and you will become an excellent listener. The rewards will be amazing on many levels.

LISTEN
Activity 2: Active Listening Techniques

The following exercise uses the key ideas from the previous page.

Practice the techniques below by watching a YouTube video or practicing with a friend. Take turns with another person to practice being a good listener.

1. Restatement: This shows that you are listening by repeating back what the person said.
    For example: "So, what you are saying is…."
    Or "OK, I understand. Your idea is…."

2. Encouragement: This keeps the person talking.
    For example: "I see…."
    Or "That's interesting…." (No need to relay your own experiences.)

3. Reflection: This shows empathy and understanding.
    For example, "You feel that…."
    Or "It made you happy that…."

4. Summarization: This shows that you understand the whole idea of what is being said.

   For example, "To summarize, you think that...."

   Or "If I understand correctly, the major concerns are...."

Practice, practice, practice.

MAKE A MEAL

A HOME-PREPARED MEAL has many advantages. The meal can be more nutritious than restaurant meals, and certainly less expensive. Beyond that, you have a chance to express your creativity. There's a real sense of fun and accomplishment. Also, making a meal is potential for more fun if others participate in the kitchen with you.

You are a flower that needs nutrients. You need good healthy food to be strong and grow. Maintaining a healthy body and mind is valuable for balance.

Create something with your hands. Get out of your mind and back into your body. Give yourself the gift of preparing a wonderful meal.

On the practical side, food consumed while dining out can be high in calories and fat. Often restaurants add artificial flavoring. It can be hard to see into the restaurant's kitchen, which may not be as clean as you would expect or may be using ingredients past their prime. And in a day when large portions are expected, it's very difficult to monitor the amount of food eaten. Good health and weight control depend on portion size.

Practical reasons aside, creativity is important to happiness. Studies indicate that people produce endorphins (happy chemicals) when doing something new for the brain. And with the vast array of cuisine and the number of recipes in print and on the Internet, you can find something new to create every day. You can experiment and learn about new cultures through food.

Cooking can be a source of joy. Personally, I like to read a recipe for the main idea, and then improvise to my taste. Feel free to experiment. You can have fun with cooking.

Many of us have service jobs that seem never ending. Often we don't get that "great job done, everyone can see my accomplishment" feeling. When you prepare a meal, you have completed a task, and you will have something great to show for it.

And meal preparation doesn't need to be time-consuming. Many meals can be cooked in twenty minutes. Crock-Pot cooking, stir frying, or grilling can be quick and easy. Buying pre-made sauces or a whole chicken and then adding ingredients around it is a good way to cut corners. Another idea is to prepare in advance and freeze your dinners. You can cook several meals on your day off and put the food away to use during the rest of the week.

It is less expensive to buy your own food and prepare it yourself. This is true even if you purchase fast food. When you buy food that is already made, you not only pay for the food itself, but for the overhead of the store or restaurant and the salary of the food preparer. For one week, take note of the cost of eating out. At the end of the week, total up the cost. You may be amazed. By preparing your own dinners, you can save even more money by brown-bagging your lunch the next day, with leftovers or a sandwich made to your personal taste.

Another benefit to preparing a meal and eating at home is the sheer social value. Sitting together and sharing a meal contributes to your family's social life. You can talk about the day with each other, get to know your family, and practice good eating habits all at the same time. Children of families that share meals are at less risk for undesirable behaviors and issues. Children who eat at home tend to earn better grades.

Twenty years ago families ate about sixty percent of their meals together. Today that number is down to twenty percent. The best item invented to encourage communication was the table.

It is a pleasure to pause and enjoy the company of others. Together we can enjoy the blessing of having physical and emotional nourishment. Sharing a prepared meal is a basic activity that may help us get more out of life. Many of us have moved away from this daily pleasure. It's time to get cooking.

Sandra had a good job and was always going out to eat. She was laid off and had to make adjustments in her budget. The first thing to cut was the eating out. She began to buy groceries and prepare her own meals. Sandra started looking up recipes online and enjoyed experimenting with different foods. She invited friends over and had potluck meals. This was fun. Sandra also lost some weight because she was able to monitor her food's fat content, nutritional value and portions. A few months passed and Sandra got another job. But she did not go back to eating out as often. She learned that preparing her own meals can be economical, fun and part of taking control of her life.

Ask yourself the following questions:

- Do you eat more than eighty percent of your meals outside of your home?
- Are most of your entertainment costs spent on meals out?
- Do you eat every meal in front of the television?
- Do you often eat standing up?
- Are you gaining weight and do not understand the reason?

If you answered yes to any of these questions, you may consider preparing more meals at home.

MAKE A MEAL
Activity 1: Foods You Enjoy

How do you start on the path to preparing home-cooked meals?

List your ten favorite foods (not necessarily in any order).

	Food	Portion	Calories per portion
1.			
2.			
3.			
4.			
5.			

	Food	Portion	Calories per portion
6.	_____		
7.	_____		
8.	_____		
9.	_____		
10.	_____		

Go back and list the portion or serving size, and the calories per serving. This is for your reference.

Using a cookbook or the Internet, research new recipes for some of your favorite meals. You may be delighted with dishes that have fewer calories or less fat but taste the same as your old recipes.

MAKE A MEAL

Activity 2: Eat Responsibly and Still Have Fun

1. Look at your list of favorite meals from Activity One. Choose three of your favorite food dishes that you think you would like to prepare.

2. Plan a meal aiming to make some of your favorites.

3. Imagine your meal.

4. Make a shopping list.

5. Do the shopping. Bring your list.

6. Make your meal.

7. Congratulate yourself on your accomplishment and enjoy your feast!

I would strongly encourage you to invite some people over and share your favorite foods with them. You may encourage your friends to think of their favorites and invite them the next month. You could cook together or perhaps do a potluck dinner.

NEEDS versus WANTS
(Simplify Your Life)

LET'S START WITH definitions. A "need" is something that you must have to survive; a "want" is something you would like to have. Acknowledging the difference between these two words actually gives you control over them rather than letting them control you.

This concept of using a product to create happiness is the core of marketing. For examples, if you use certain toothpaste, drive a specific type of car, or wear the same clothes as a movie star — you too will be a star.

We would all like to be rich. Or at least, we want to have enough money to feel secure and comfortable. But exactly how much is enough? Five million dollars? Ten million?

We are truly rich when we are content with what we have now.

Wants and needs are taught early and go very deep. We learn as a child how to be a consumer. Parents are begged, coaxed and threatened to buy things by advertisers and advertiser-programmed children. Commercials promise parents items that will make their kids smarter, stronger and better. Toddlers are dazzled with fantasy worlds of happy people inside fast food restaurants.

We actually perpetuate these commercial-generated wants in the language we use. Consider the statement, "I need a Mercedes Benz." It means that I need this for survival. However, if I say "I want a Mercedes Benz," I just show a desire. I won't perish from the lack of it.

One experience that taught me "need" versus "want" was when I decided to study in another city. It was a three-month trip, and I could only take with me what I could fit in the car. At first it was difficult not having all the things I prefer to use or wear. But after a week, it was easy. Actually, it was easier than having all of my stuff. Cleaning was easier, things were easier to find, and simplifying my life was refreshing.

If you desire more and more, you will not be happy with yourself. Yes, there are certain necessities in life, but these are fairly basic. How much more than food and shelter do we really need?

And food can be bread and cheese purchased from the grocery store. We do not need to pay twenty times the price to eat the same food in an expensive restaurant.

There is nothing wrong with wanting things — in fact want can be a great motivator. But when you get it into your mind that you *must* have this thing to survive, you lose your power. The desire controls you.

Also, too much desire may be a source of depression or anxiety. We feel we cannot get what we want, which makes us depressed and feeling worthless. Life seems hopeless. We cannot be what we would like to be.

The anxiety aspect comes into play when we worry about the future and confuse what we would like to have with what we truly need. We worry that we must get a better job so we can buy more things. We stress over all the "wants" that we think we should have.

We not only feel bad because we don't have the Mercedes; deep down we start to believe it is our fault. We have done something wrong.

Therefore, separating the "needs" from the "wants" is helpful to stay in balance. We will be more emotionally stable if we differentiate between the two and seek only what we truly need rather than what we want. Focusing on needs rather than wants may free up time to focus more on the physical and spiritual sides of life.

It is so seductive to go after all the wants in our lives. But we need to keep it in proper perspective. Think about the words "need" and "want." Which of our wants do we truly desire, and which are old programmed ideas long out of date?

You can benefit from re-evaluating your needs and wants.

- Are you spending more than you earn?
- Are you always online looking at things?
- Do you worry about being able to buy the things you want?
- Do you go to stores and buy things impulsively?
- Do you think you will never have the life you want?
- Do you believe that if you only had more things, your life would be so much better?

If you answered "yes" to any of these questions, then do the following activities.

NEEDS versus WANTS
Activity 1: Simplify Your Life

It is valuable to simplify your life.

Look around your home. Think about each item — could you live life without it? Set a goal to eliminate one third of your possessions. Doing so removes the clutter and makes it easier to clean and manage your home.

Use this same process to go through your clothes and accessories. One rule that people use to decide which clothes to eliminate is: If an item has not been worn for a year, it likely will not be used and should be removed.

Give these possessions to charity. It's a gift to pass along these items to somebody who can really use them.

NEEDS versus WANTS
Activity 2

Let's think about what we really want versus what we really need. Answer the questions below about activities in which people frequently engage. For those activities that apply to you, list the average cost of participation.

Average
Cost

List how many times per month you go out
for coffee: _____   _____

List how many times per month you go out
to eat: _____   _____

Do you smoke cigarettes? How many
per week? _____   _____

How many sweets do you buy and/or eat
in a week? _____   _____

How often do you go shopping
for clothes? _____   _____

How often do you buy items that are
not necessities? _____   _____

	Average Cost
How much do you spend per month on liquor? _____	_____
How much do you spend per month on going out for entertainment? _____	_____

The above items are "wants," not necessities. How many of those items do you truly desire? Do you really enjoy every moment of doing these activities?

For which items do you feel the time and money could be better spent?

Let's find out how much time and money you really spend on these items. Create a log of when and how often the above behaviors occur. Write down the dollar amount and time spent. Isn't it amazing how much we spend on wants that are not necessary?

But we can improve! How can you cut back on your desires that take your time and money? Write down a list of actions you can do to reduce the time and money spent on some of these things.

(If you try, and a month later you are not at all successful, you may have impulsivity issues that may require professional counseling.)

OBSTACLES
(Quitting)

LIFE HAS OBSTACLES. Sometimes the obstacle is a problem to solve. Sometimes the obstacle is a road block indicating the need to go in another direction.

It is not the problems or obstacles in our lives that are the isssue, but rather how we deal with these problems.

As an adult, it is your turn to make **your** choices. You may encounter obstacles in achieving what you want.

Here's an example.

Many of us are told from early childhood what we should be when we grow up. Parents and grandparents may dream of their child's success as a surgeon; the media broadcasts the brilliant life of actors; coaches urge youngsters toward being great athletes. Teachers, peers, relatives — virtually all the people we meet — have strong ideas of what we should grow up to be. The best baseball player, the prettiest girl, the best pianist or the smartest student in the class are all held up as ideals.

Progress is just giving yourself permission to think about what you truly want and not what others may want for you. Sometimes you may be doing things for the money. You may have been convinced that a bigger house, a fancier car, a thinner self, or glamorous clothes will make you feel complete and content. But the reality is that the rich and famous celebrities have problems also.

John was a Senior in high school. His parents were always pushing him to get excellent grades and become a doctor. This was his obstacle. John could not get A's no matter how hard he tried. The truth was that he had an undiagnosed learning disability. In the summers, he would work construction jobs and he enjoyed this profession. But his parents would not hear about a career in the construction field. John became frustrated and depressed. He began doing drugs. Shortly thereafter, he overdosed and died.

It is not healthy to wake up every morning and dread getting out of bed to face your day. If you can't change your job or living situation, you may be able to add something to your life that you do enjoy and look forward to doing. Start making choices for yourself — to enjoy your life.

When do you persevere and when do you move on to something new? Let's look at Molly, a seventh grade student and a victim of bullying. She went through the experiences of harsh name calling and being left out of groups in school. Her parents met with the teachers. The administration brought in specialists to facilitate an anti-bullying program. At the end of the school year, they promised it would be better.

However, on the first day of the next school year, Molly was pushed and called names. Her mother said, "Enough. It is time to put you in a different school." After all, for a full school year they had tried everything the school had suggested — yet nothing had changed. And indeed, Molly did very well in her new school.

After you have tried to make a situation better but nothing has improved, it may be time to try a different path. You have the power to change. You can choose a different relationship, job or place to live.

There are times when you need to solve the challenge — to address an issue. And there are times when you need to walk away.

How do you know if it is time to quit the situation rather than persevere?

- You wish that what you are doing was already finished. You look forward to your time away from the challenge much more than when you are in the given situation.

- There does not seem to be any gain. Sometimes you may be throwing good money after bad trying to recoup your losses.

- You do not enjoy anything about the situation and there is no change or end in sight.

- Your priorities, goals and/or lifestyles have changed. This situation is no longer filling any of your needs or wants.

- You are trying to push forward in an unpleasant situation to please someone else — a parent, a child, a spouse. But for you there is no joy in this negative situation.

If you answered yes to any of the above questions, try the following activities. You might also try the Sort activity in the "D" or "Decision Making" section.

OBSTACLES
Activity 1: Analyzing Your Obstacles

Brainstorm a list of obstacles you face right now?

_____

_____

_____

_____

_____

Now, go down the list and answer each question.

    1.   Define the exact obstacle.

_____

_____

_____

_____

_____

2. Is the obstacle a problem that can be pushed through to a solution, or is it something you don't want to do but feel you must?

_____

_____

_____

_____

_____

3. If resolved, what will your new situation be?

_____

_____

_____

_____

_____

4. How would you feel about this resolution?

_____

_____

_____

_____

_____

5. If you do nothing about this obstacle, what will your life look like?

_____

_____

_____

_____

_____

6. Is this similar to a problem you've experienced in the past? Reoccurring problems may mean there's a deeper issue that must be addressed.

_____

_____

_____

_____

_____

7. Now think about this carefully: Will you be truly happier to walk away, or will you be truly happier to have changed or conquered it?

_____

_____

_____

_____

_____

OBSTACLES
Activity 2: Evaluate Your Life

Look in the mirror and ask yourself what you truly want to change. Write your answers below. Note: You may fill in only a few of these, or you may add a category yourself.

Habit

a. _____

b. _____

c. _____

Behavior

a. _____

b. _____

c. _____

Work and/or school

    a. _____

    b. _____

    c. _____

Attitude

    a. _____

    b. _____

    c. _____

Now, look at your list. Below, write next to the letter how you plan to make the change.

Example: Habit. a. biting nails. I plan to buy nasty tasing nail polish and put on my nails to prevent me from biting.

Example: Behavior. a. I interrupt too much. I am going to count to 3 before I say something in a conversation.

Habit

    a. _____

    b. _____

    c. _____

Behavior

    a. _____

    b. _____

    c. _____

Work and/or school

    a. _____

    b. _____

    c. _____

Attitude

    a. _____

    b. _____

    c. _____

Play is important

Play has many benefits. Play gives the mind and the body a break from the daily grind. Play is also a good way to have fun with other people, to create and feel challenged.

Play benefits your emotional side as well. By taking the time to relax from your normal routine, play helps you become more balanced. You feel more at ease with yourself. Psychologically, play brings you to a place of fun and releases endomorphins. These endomorphins lift your mood, helping to alleviate pain, fear and worry. Play is great for stress release.

Physical play, such as tennis or racquetball, is excellent for maintaining good health. These activities exercise the muscles, the cardiovascular system and the brain. Studies indicate that physical exercise actually helps maintain brain function. Blood flow to the brain increases, keeping the blood vessels strong.

Play helps you to focus and facilitates being in the present. You cannot win a tennis match if you are not focusing on the ball. Neither can you shine at work if you are not truly focused on the task before you. You need to "keep your eye on the ball." Playing helps you stay in the here and now. (See chapter on "Joy in the Present").

Play also teaches perseverance. The reward of mastering a new game reinforces to the body and brain that perseverance pays off. We have the opportunity to try new things without negative consequences. Play allows us to experiment and then apply what we have learned to life.

Playtime is every bit as essential for adults as it is for children.

Play is basic and natural. It helps us to survive by connecting with others and providing pleasure for ourselves. It's positive activity for our body and brain.

As a child, playing develops and improves social skills. We learn to give and take, to wait for our turn. We learn to watch and understand others. We learn how to live and work in a community. Verbal communication and body language, safety and danger, freedom and boundaries, cooperation and teamwork — all are discovered and honed through play. Play stimulates our curiosity, our imagination, and helps us to solve problems. It is a chance to try activities without the permanence of real life.

All these skills need to be maintained and expanded as adults. Playing is a part of staying in balance, since play affects our emotional, cognitive, spiritual and of course, physical sides.

Eva had a career that took up many hours a week. Once off work, she would go home and rest because she was so tired. Eva's niece joined a basketball team. She asked Eva to go and practice basketball with her. Eva told her that she was too busy. Then Eva remembered growing up and how she had always wanted to play ball, but nobody had time for her. She recalled that emotional pain. So, Eva agreed to meet with her niece once a week to shoot baskets and practice one-on-one. Eva soon started to look forward to their play time. She grew closer with her niece. After a couple of months, Eva joined a league herself and made some new friends. Playing opened up her life.

The opposite of play is not work — it's depression. When we play with others we're reminded that we're not alone. Loneliness is lessened. Even watching a game with other people is advantageous. Just getting out and being with people is important.

Play is an important aspect of having a balanced life. It is as valuable to play as it is to work and rest.

Play also teaches us about winning and losing. We need to accept both as part of life. We can't always win!

If you are not doing something fun and creative for five hours a week, you're losing a key ingredient of a healthy life.

You may want to do the following activities.

PLAY

Activity 1: Brainstorm about Play

List some of the games you enjoyed as a child.

1. _____

2. _____

3. _____

4. _____

5. _____

6. _____

7. _____

8. _____

Go through the list and ask yourself if these games are possible to play as an adult. Write "yes" or "no" beside each game.

For those games for which you answered "yes," think about where and when you could enjoy this activity again and with whom.

Write them here:

_____

_____

_____

_____

_____

_____

_____

_____

_____

_____

_____

_____

_____

_____

_____

_____

PLAY
Activity 2: Let's Have Fun

Make time to play.

In Activity 1, you thought of activities you enjoyed as a child and determined which games you could play as an adult, where and when you could play these activities, and with whom. Look at your list again.

List some activities for play that you have not tried before. Add these to your list (for example, the Wii or joining a card club).

_____

_____

_____

_____

_____

Try to set aside a half an hour per day to play. This could be cumulative for the week. Play time may be a good activity on your rest day.

Now, go and have some fun!

A B C D E F G H I J K L M N O P **Q** R S T U V W X Y Z

QUESTION AND LEARN ALWAYS

IT IS IMPORTANT to learn, and there are many reasons for engaging in continued education.

To question is to seek knowledge, to explore, to understand and to participate.

Why should you ask "why?" Through this one-word question, we can determine the cause of things. One way to keep the search for truth alive by asking "why?" and refusing to just accept the ideas that are handed to us.

Questioning is important. At one point everyone believed that the world was flat; if one sailed too far, the ship would fall off the earth. There are many popular beliefs today that scientific tests have failed to verify. One of these is that sugar causes hyperactivity. The results of many double-blind studies indicate there is not evidence to show that sugar will cause increased hyperactivity. A comprehensive double blind study was published in the *Journal of American Medical Association* in 1995 (Welraish, Wilson, White) where half the children were given food with sugar and half were given food with artificial sweeteners. Neither the children nor the observers knew who had what. The children who consumed the sugar were no more or less active than the children without the sugar. The human body will process sugar evenly unless you are diabetic or hypoglycemic. You may ask and should ask, "WHY do people hold onto this belief?" People want simple answers to comply with their behavior. For example, it is easy to blame the bakery that used too much sugar in the cake for a children's' party that got out of control. I witnessed a grandmother scolding the bakery clerk because she claimed that the birthday cake had too much sugar. Therefore, the children were wild and the party a disaster.

So, how does one navigate in this world? The compass and map are available through life-long learning, which means continuous learning about many things using many sources.

As Mark Twain said, "I never let my schooling get in the way of my education."

Continuing education means self-development; aimed at strengthening your emotional and spiritual sides. Through learning we grow. A flower needs nourishment to grow. Knowledge is nourishment. With knowledge we also bloom.

It is valuable to get information from written word and other sources. We are privileged to live in a free society. Freedom of speech is a rare commodity for most people in the world, and one that we should not take for granted. Instead, take advantage of the gift of freedom of speech. Get different perspectives from multiple sources, by reading, listening to the radio and watching television. It is valuable to understand others.

Historically, many people have been murdered as a result of simple answers and scapegoats. The Crusaders thought that the world's problems were caused by non-Christians. The Nazis taught that the Jews were the cause of problems with the world economy and that the world would be a better place if the Jews were destroyed. The Taliban preaches that Infidels (anyone not them) need to be destroyed to save the world. But the reality is that tolerance is critical to world peace. Tolerance is taught by understanding and respecting the viewpoints of others. We must look at all viewpoints and not take the position of, "Don't confuse me with the facts; I've already made up my mind." Instead get the facts and decide for yourself.

Therefore it is vital to ask questions. I believe our media is biased and does not give us the entire truth. Even the Internet is skewed to your likes and dislikes. For example, if you search on the word "Egypt," your search will result in a different set of websites (and ads!) than if I search "Egypt" on my computer. For marketing purposes, Google and others keep track of what we are interested in based on the searches we have performed on our home or office computers, and show us only the websites that they feel contain information that fits our interests. For example, because you do frequent searches on travel destinations and read articles and subscribe to blogs about travel, you may get vacation sites as a result of your query about Egypt. Because I tend to read a lot of articles from various sources about the politics in Egypt, my query results in websites that deal with Mideast politics. The problem here is that the search engine sways our opinions by limiting the information to which we are exposed.

We need to question what is opinion and what is fact? "Fact" is something that has scientific evidence; "the world is round" is a fact. Opinion is a belief or judgment that is held firmly but without actual proof of its truth. In my view, far too often we hear statements and accept them as fact, when in reality the statements are merely opinions. Instead, we should stop and think about the assumptions of statements. What is the source? What is their bias? Is this statement sound? Would this be universally true? Why is this being presented?

People have a tendency to make quick judgments and label others. One of the defense mechanisms in psychology is called splitting. In this theory, the individual views other people and things as either all good or all bad. Much like the world from the perspective of a two-year-old, there is no in between. All good and all bad is like the world being either black or white. But look around. The world has some black and some white but mostly it has colors: blue, red, green and more. Individuals and situations are also this way. Nobody is all good or all bad. I know it can be scary and difficult to think about others more broadly. But if we want to expand our minds and reach out, we must treat others as we want to be treated. This includes trying to learn and understand about other nations, cultures, political beliefs and opinions.

Learning also has benefits for our professional lives. We can get ahead at work if we study more. We may even get into the career that we have always wanted by getting a better education.

Finally, life-long learning and asking questions will help develop your intellectual side. It is important to stay balanced with the four sides of yourself: cognitive, spiritual, emotional and physical. If you have a passion or interest in a particular area, learn more about it. The world is constantly changing and we need to learn in order to keep up. Take a class. Join a club or group. Ideas that you learn can become good conversation topics. Also, studies have shown that our brains produce endomorphones (happy hormones) when we are challenged by learning new things. Learning helps your brain stay young by being active.

Jasper thought that he had no future growing up in a poor part of town. He never knew his father, and his mother worked two jobs to try to keep the bills paid and support two children. While a sophomore in high school, he decided to help out and get a part-time job after school. He began to work in a local pharmacy. The owner/pharmacist was always reading. Jasper was curious and would ask him questions. Jasper began to ask his teachers questions. He began to read on his own. His grades became all A's. Jasper received a scholarship to college. He enjoyed learning even more. Jasper became a teacher himself and gives back to his community to inspire youth to learn and grow.

It is important to challenge yourself. We learn and then we grow.

- Do you believe everything you hear or read?
- Are you reacting and making judgments based on information received from one source?
- Are you learning something new every day?
- Do you think about how you are feeling about a situation and why?
- Do you know the names of your mayor and governor? Do you know what they have been doing or not doing?
- Do you wonder why things work?
- Would you like to change to a job that might require you to be trained in a different field?
- Are you retired or thinking about retiring and would like to start a hobby?

Then question, learn and you will grow!

QUESTION AND LEARN
Activity 1

The following are suggestions for cultivating life-long learning:

Check off the ones that you would like to do.

- ☐ Always have a book or an article on the go. You don't have to have a deadline to finish reading something. But if you have a few minutes, it is good to have something to read.

- ☐ Keep a "to learn list." Post the list as a motivator.

- ☐ Process what you are learning and reading. Try to journal and/ or talk to others about what you have been studying.

- ☐ Put into practice: "I hear and forget, I see and remember, I do and understand." — Confucius

This is important because we learn what we do. If you have read about painting, then pick up a brush and start doing.

- ☐ Teach others. You learn when you teach because you have to know a subject well enough to communicate the ideas to others. Start a blog, mentor somebody, tutor or just discuss ideas with others.

☐ Learn in groups. Join a study group, book club, or a class. You are more prone to attend and process when doing with other people.

☐ Start a new hobby, even collecting family photos and writing down names and dates. Ask family members to help.

☐ Unlearn assumptions. Try to look at ideas from a fresh perspective. Try to stop and think about the viewpoint of others.

☐ Aim for rewards. Learn things that may advance your job or career.

☐ Make learning a priority by setting aside time to learn. Look at your weekly schedule and plan fifteen minutes a day for learning, if possible. Schedule time for this just like exercising or relaxing. Make it a part of your day. Make learning a part of who you are!

QUESTION AND LEARN

Activity 1: Making a Plan to Improve Yourself Through Learning

A.   Write a list of things you would like to learn.

    1.   Example: Learn Spanish

    2.   _____

    3.   _____

    4.   _____

    5.   _____

(You can list more, if you like.)

B. How are you going to learn these things? Example: Buy a book, join a class, read Internet articles, watch YouTube videos.... By the way, it is better to learn with somebody else. Find a partner who is also interested in expanding his or her mind.

1. Example: Learn Spanish. Join a community college class with my friend Alice.

2. _____

3. _____

4. _____

5. _____

C. Now put a time on this goal of learning.

1. Example: Learn Spanish at community college with Alice starting this fall semester at night.

2. _____

3. _____

4. _____

5. _____

REST AND RELAXATION TIME

SET ASIDE ONE DAY a week for rest and relaxation.

You may be thinking, "I do not have the time to take off and still get everything done." You will never find time unless you create time. We make choices. Make a choice to have balance in your life.

If you can't do a whole day of rest and relaxation, then set aside a few hours a week. Try to make it the same time each week as your body and mind will be ready for this rest. It is a time to recharge.

The body requires rest mentally and physically, and one day a week gives us the time to recharge. If we are constantly working, we do not have a chance to focus our attention on ourselves, family and friends — to remind us why we work, and to enjoy the current fruits of our labor. Set this time aside for being in the moment, for truly relaxing.

Nobody on his or her death bed ever said, "I should have spent more time in the office."

Actually, a break makes us more productive when we do get back to school or work.

The idea of a day of rest was introduced in the Bible, and was a new concept at the time. The ancient Egyptians and Babylonians did not have a day off. In the Bible, this day of rest was extended to slaves and livestock. The land itself even had a Sabbatical every seven years to let it replenish and become more fertile. All living things need a time to rest and regroup.

This concept of having a day of rest may be called the Sabbath. In Hebrew, "Sabbath" means "cessation" or "to stop." It is not so much about what you do as what you do NOT do. Avoid errands and the usual running around if that is what is do during the week. Be with friends and family. Have a meal. Picnic in the park. Go for a walk. Watch a movie or a TV program. Do something enjoyable.

We can also take this opportunity to get unplugged from all the technology. Today we are constantly connected. What would happen if we did not have the Internet, cell phones or television? We could talk to each other face-to-face without interruption. We could play cards or board games and relate. We could go for a walk or enjoy outdoor activities with the family.

On the first Friday of the month my family has a "family and friends night". I make a dinner. We clear the laptop and papers from the dining room table and set it. The meal is made more special by having it in the dining room. We usually play music and we all sing. We often play a board game and enjoy the fun. It is a pleasant way to spend an evening. We talk, sing and visit.

Knowing that we are taking a day off forces us to prepare for it. It's like preparing to go away on a trip. We need to think about what we will get done before, and what can wait until after. So it's also about self-denial and self-discipline. Also, waiting for this day of rest is delayed gratification. These are all useful skills to practice.

The truth is we can get so caught up in the race that we can't stop running. We need time to learn, pray, and be with others in the community. It is a matter of running your life and not letting your life run you. If you can't find a day to relax, find a few hours. Start small and work your way up.

Relaxation time facilitates balance as it is tied into the spiritual part. By giving ourselves time to rest and connect to others and the world, we renew the spirit.

Also, this rest time helps maintain the balance of our spiritual, cognitive, emotional and physical parts. It helps to nourish the flower that is you, so you can bloom.

Take some time for yourself. Take a day to stop your usual routine and just enjoy life. You will reap the benefits.

- Do you feel like your life is non-stop?
- Is your life running you instead of you running it?
- Do you want to spend more time doing activities for enjoyment?

If yes, set aside a specific scheduled time each week to rest and relax. Put it in your calendar.

REST AND RELAXATION TIME
Activity 1: Plan Your Day

If you are having trouble thinking of things to do, here are some ideas.

- Celebrate family and friends. Have people over to the house or go to others' homes.

- Interview older members of the family or senior friends about history. Look at family albums or movies.

- Do community service.

- Read together.

- Go for a walk.

- Paint, garden, ride a bike.

- Meditate.

- Go to a lecture.

- Attend a service.

- Have friends or family to your home

- Go out to eat

- Stay home and prepare a meal and then enjoy with others

– Do a hobby

– Catch up with friends and family on the phone or Facebook or better in person

REST AND RELAXATION TIME

Activity 2: Make a plan for Rest and Relaxation Time

1. Choose a time of the week, that you could set aside for Rest and Relaxation Time

   _____

2. Make a list of items you would like to do at this time.

   _____

   _____

   _____

   _____

   _____

   _____

   _____

3. Keep a log of what you did

_____

_____

_____

_____

_____

_____

4. How did you feel?

_____

_____

_____

_____

5. What would you change for the next time?

_____

_____

_____

_____

6. Change or add to your list of things to do on Rest and Relaxation Time list.

7. Continue this process of finding your Rest and Relaxation Time and what is good for you to enjoy this special time.

SLEEP

SLEEP IS AN ACTIVE PROCESS that is essential for mental and physical well-being.

We often believe that sleep is a waste of time. We give it a low priority when compared to all the other things in our days. There is so much to do, we think, so why waste time sleeping it away?

Think again! Sleep is a priority.

Sleep is essential for our bodies, including the immune system, the nervous system, development and hormone stability. Without adequate sleep, the immune system weakens. We are more likely to become ill mentally and physically. The body can only work so hard and if it does not have enough sleep it uses vital energy just to sustain normalcy, making us less immune to disease.

One study showed people who slept less than six hours were four times more likely to develop abnormal blood sugar readings or diabetic symptoms compared with those who slept longer. Other studies have shown that children and adults with too little sleep have an increased risk of obesity, depression and high blood pressure. In older adults, lack of sleep increases the risk of falls. In middle-aged adults, sleep deprivation raises the risk of infections, heart disease, stroke and cancer.

Sleep is also a time of rest for the nervous system. When we sleep, the neurons — the pathways connecting parts of the body to the brain — have a chance to repair. Neurons involve both voluntary and involuntary commands, from breathing to raising your arms.

The brain is rejuvenated during sleep. The brain has time to repair cellular damage and even grow new nerve cells. Hormones that regulate body functions and moods are timed to release during sleep or right before sleep.

Sleep also allows our muscles to rest. Sleep can help heal a strained back or legs. The body has a natural tendency to get well if we give it the opportunity to rejuvenate.

Sleep deprivation is dangerous to you and to others. Lack of sleep affects motor skills, which are needed for many tasks including driving a car. The US National Highway Traffic Safety Administration estimates that over one hundred thousand crashes annually are due to sleep deprivation, accounting for about fifteen fatalities and seventy-one thousand injuries.

Lack of sleep affects our relationships and performance on the job or at school. It affects our mood and judgment. We tend to be more agitated when sleep-deprived. We do not think well when we are tired. Excessive sleepiness contributes to a twofold risk of sustaining an injury on the job.

Studies have shown that reducing your sleep by as little as one and a half hours for just one night could result in a thirty-two percent reduction of daytime alertness.

Sleep is intertwined with all our systems and without it we may feel out of balance. We need adequate sleep for our cognitive side. We cannot think well or focus without enough rest. Sleep is important for the physical side, as it impacts our nervous system, our muscles, our hormones and our metabolism. Emotionally, we have all had the experience of saying things out of anger or feeling anxious or depressed because we didn't get enough sleep. Also, the spiritual side cannot be pursued and enjoyed to its fullest without adequate sleep. Overall, sleep is connected to our well-being.

Jake lived to socialize. He never shut it down. He "facebooked" and texted all the time. Although he was getting seven hours of sleep a night, his sleep was often interrupted by texting notifications or friends calling just to chat. Jake studied hard in college, but his grades were C's or worse. He was afraid to tell his parents that he may be flunking some of his classes. He also found himself to be short-tempered. Then one day in psychology class, the professor spoke about sleep and the value to the cognitive process. The professor also talked about emotions. Jake decided to do an experiment on himself. He turned off his phone at night. He slept a solid eight hours. The next day, he found it easy to focus and he felt good. Jake realized that by unplugging at night he was more "plugged-in" to his day.

Naps are beneficial. Don't feel guilty about taking a power nap. Taking a nap is a good way to recharge. I can testify that a twenty-minute nap allows me to function well into the night.

How do you know if you are sleep-deprived? Children from ages six to nine need approximately ten hours of sleep, ages nine to eighteen need nine hours, and adults approximately eight hours of sleep.

The following are signs that you may be suffering sleep deprivation.

- Difficulty waking up in the morning
- Poor performance in school or on the job
- Increased clumsiness
- Difficulty making decisions
- Falling asleep during work or class
- Feeling especially moody or irritated
- Having trouble concentrating
- Having difficulty remembering things

SLEEP
Activity 1

The following will help insure your good night's rest.

Review these and think about what you would like to improve or do.

FOODS THAT CAN INTERFERE WITH SLEEP

☐ Too much food, especially fatty or rich food. Your stomach may have to work hard to digest this food. You may get heartburn or stomach problems which are worse when lying down.

☐ Too much liquid. About four hours before bedtime, stop drinking. If you take in liquid within four hours of going to bed, you may need to get up to use the bathroom and therefore have interrupted sleep.

☐ Alcohol. Alcohol may make you feel tired, but it can interfere with sleep and cause frequent awakenings.

☐ Caffeine. Avoid foods like coffee, chocolate and tea several hours before going to sleep. Caffeine is a drug that is a stimulant.

818 | *Life from A to Z*

YOUR BED AND BEDDING

☐ Make sure your bed is a good size for you. It should be large enough to let you stretch out and turn freely. If your mattress is too hard, you could buy a foam topper for additional softness.

☐ Your bedding is important. Soft sheets and pillowcases can add a cozy feeling. Fleece blankets are wonderful to snuggle into and go to sleep.

YOUR ROOM

☐ Temperature and ventilation are important. If your room is too warm, consider a fan to keep the air circulating. Some people like to sleep when it is warm and some when it is cooler. Experiment to see what temperature suits you the best.

☐ Keep your room dark during sleeping hours. You may want to get shades or blinds to keep the room dark at night and in the morning until wake-up time.

☐ Keep your room as quiet as possible. If there is noise that you cannot control (such as an old furnace or the neighbor's dog) try ear plugs. A fan or soothing music may provide white noise to cover the sound.

☐ Reserve your bed for sleeping. If you use your bed for doing work, your subconscious may associate the bed with work and therefore stress.

After looking at the preceding suggestions, are there any changes that you would like to make? What are they?

_____

_____

_____

_____

_____

_____

_____

_____

_____

_____

_____

_____

_____

_____

SLEEP

Activity 2: How to Organize Better Bedtime Routine

It is important to develop a relaxing bedtime routine. When performed every night, your body will get into a rhythm and cooperate more easily with going to sleep. It is suggested to go to bed and wake up at the same time every day. You body will get into this rhythm.

> Start with calculating what time you need to get up in order to start your day. Count backwards eight hours (the recommended amount of sleep for the average adult) to arrive at your suggested bedtime.

> An hour before your bedtime, start getting ready for sleep. Think about what relaxes you. It might be a warm bath, a good book, soft music, etc.

> Avoid bright lights, loud music and activities that may cause stress or anxiety (as much as is realistically possible).

> Avoid reading negative books or watching the news in this hour prior to sleep. Instead, watch a funny show or read something relaxing.

You may want to do a peaceful activity, such as stretching or yoga.

Whatever activities you choose, do them each night before going to bed. Your body and mind will start to get the cues. Going to sleep becomes a natural flow of behaviors.

Write your ideal bedtime routine.

_____

_____

_____

_____

_____

_____

Try this routine for a week then make changes as needed.

THANKFULNESS

THANKFULNESS MEANS counting your blessings. It's noticing simple pleasures and being grateful for what you have.

The best attitude is having gratitude.

Thankfulness means learning to live your life as though it were a gift.

Thankfulness helps you keep things in perspective. It facilitates thinking about what is important. When you focus on what you lack, there is a tendency to complain and feel depressed. But it's hard to complain about doing housework when you are grateful to have a home. When I find myself annoyed with having to clean the kitchen all the time, I say "thanks" for having a kitchen.

Gratitude shifts your focus from what your life lacks, to what you do have. Think about that. Recognizing what you are thankful for puts things in a positive light. Rather than dwelling on the negative, you look at what is right in your life.

Giving thanks makes people happier and stronger and can strengthen relationships. Gratitude reduces stress and improves mental and physical well-being.

A philosophical question: Who are happy?

Answer: Those that are content with what they have.

How does gratitude strengthen relationships? When we take the time to thank others, we show that we care, which can lead to others reciprocating and letting us know that they care about us. It is a circle circulating with gratitude.

Thankfulness helps our emotional side. It makes us feel that we are needed. Gratitude allows us to reach out and nurture our friends and family and those who may become our friends and family. Being grateful aids our balance in life.

People often regret not showing thankfulness. "I would give anything to let them know that I love them. But it is too late." Take the time to be grateful and let others know that you appreciate them. Let your spouse, children and parents know. Don't assume they already understand. Say the words "I love you." and "Thank you". It will make a positive difference.

In a relationship, thankfulness is an amazing bonus. Just saying "thank you" to others makes you feel good towards others — and helps them feel good as well. It feels great to do something nice for others and give them a reason to smile. Look for opportunities to say "thank you" to somebody. It's amazing the real miracles that can be gained by sharing genuine gratitude.

There are many stories about being grateful. Here is one. A sixteen-year-old boy, Trevor was told that he had cancer in his leg. The only way he would live was to have it amputated. Trevor and his family were devastated. But they went ahead with the surgery and therapy. Trevor got a prosthetic leg and learned how to be mobile. He has lived a normal life and excelled. Trevor realized that he was fortunate to be alive. He decided to show others his success by doing walk-a-thons and fundraising for cancer research. He also studied and worked hard and became a successful chef. Trevor has done outreach to other cancer survivors and let them know that they should be grateful and appreciate the world around them.

People like being appreciated for who they are and what they do. Telling others you are grateful to them spreads joy.

If you are grateful for what you have, you will be less likely to feel sorry for yourself and less likely to be depressed. Being grateful for what you have allows you to be in the present and feel good about where you are now.

How do you know if you need to work on being more thankful? Consider the following questions.

- Do you tend to complain more than say positive statements?
- After you leave a social situation, are you more depressed or anxious than when you arrived?
- Do you always see yourself as a victim?
- Are you spending more time being critical of others than being positive?
- Do you feel down about your life?

If you answered "yes" to some of these, then being more thankful would be beneficial.

THANKFULNESS
Activity 1: Become Grateful

Get a notebook.

On the cover write "My Blessings." Each day or night (whenever it is convenient for you) date the top of the page and list at least three blessings — three things that you are thankful for.

If, to start, you can't think of anything, consider these blessings.

I am blessed that I can use my arms.

I am blessed that I can read.

I am blessed that I ate today.

I am blessed that I have a brother.

Continue this exercise every day.

THANKFULNESS
Activity 2: Active Gratitude

Focus on being grateful and positive day to day, even moment to moment. Here are some ways of being actively grateful.

Each day, be aware of anything negative you say. Write it down. You may want to carry a note card in your pocket.

Focus on being thankful.

Say "thank you" to others.

Make a point to call, e-mail or write a thank you letter for good service to an individual or his or her supervisor.

Look for opportunities to reciprocate favors.

Provide ways to support others less fortunate.

Send a card to say "thank you" or "thinking of you."

Stop and listen to the world around you. Be grateful for what you have.

Stop and see what is around you. Breathe and be grateful that you can breathe.

Any time you are grateful, write it down. Later you can smile and feel good about all you have.

Use your hands

THERE IS A POWER in creation and a deep satisfaction in making something.

This power of creation is extended to all creative efforts: dance, music, singing and other activities.

In today's society, many of us have service jobs, where there is no physical accomplishment to show for our efforts. Often our work seems to never be complete — we're always addressing client issues or fixing the next problem that comes along. Even when we complete a task, we rarely have anything to show for it. We're on to the next "to do" item on the list.

Also, many of us spend too much time in our heads and not in the physical world. We need a bridge back to the physical world, back to being in the moment. Doing something with our hands helps us focus on the present. For example, when we draw pictures, play musical instruments, or garden, we have to focus on the task. Using our hands facilitates balance in our lives by facilitating us to be in the present.

Creating or doing things with our hands is valuable. There's a gratification that comes from creating something that can be seen. There's a sense of accomplishment, a feeling of completion. There is something concrete to show for our efforts — to ourselves and to others. We can feel good and complete after doing something with our hands.

A hobby by definition is something that is done for pleasure — and frequently using one's hands. Painting, collecting, sewing, knitting, photography, and making models are common hobbies. Very often these activities give the opportunity to socialize and be with others. It is fun to exchange ideas, take classes, join groups or get our current friends/family involved. It is something that we can share. You might want to sew, do carpentry, paint or cook meals.

Using your hands can ultimately be a source of pride and give a sense of accomplishment — something to show for your efforts, even if it is just for you.

I held a managerial position for many years. At the end of the day, my desk might be clear. But what did I have to show for my daily efforts? Little of the work was tangible. However, when I created something with my hands, I looked at it and felt pride. I feel positive about doing something that I can touch and see.

A friend started a needle point. It took her six months to finish. To reward herself and her long effort, she had it professionally framed. Now it is displayed next to her computer like a first-place prize to commemorate her accomplishment. It makes her smile whenever she sees it.

Also, creating something and then giving it to others may give both parties much joy. My house is decorated with things that were created by my children, friends and family members. I get much pleasure from seeing these things and remembering the people who created them.

Doing something with your hands can reduce stress. A friend of mine tends to be anxious and worry about the future. When that happens, she takes out a drawing pad. Drawing helps her focus on something other than her worries. The art is fun and gives her a sense of accomplishment.

For myself, I enjoy watching television but feel that I am wasting my time. However, if I do needlework or sew while I am watching television, I can still enjoy my show and feel productive.

By creating with our hands, we may be less judgmental and more accepting. At work we berate ourselves for a project that went less than perfect. We notice every flaw. But we can marvel at that first pottery vase, amazed at what we accomplished. We learn to appreciate the hard work that goes into creating something.

Using your hands can be very gratifying. It helps you to be in the present. Using your hand can facilitate all the sides of yourself. Using your physical side fosters balance. The emotional side is benefitted by feeling good about yourself and your accomplishments. The act of creating something may lead to more social connections. You can take pride and boost your self-esteem by displaying your creative work either on a shelf or in a show.

The spiritual side is benefitted by feeling at peace with yourself. The cognitive side is used when you do a project with your hands; you may need to research the project and you have to think about what you are doing and perhaps modify your plan as you go along. The physical side is helped by doing something physical and using your body. Therefore, by using your hands, you create a balance, which helps that flower of you, blossom.

- Can you benefit from using your hands?
- Would you like to feel like you have accomplished something?

- Would you like to do something concrete with other people?
- Do you have a project or art piece that you have wanted to do?

If you answered "yes" to any of these questions, then go use your hands.

USE YOUR HANDS
Activity 1: Starting to Create

Make a list of things that you enjoy doing with your hands.

_____

_____

_____

_____

_____

_____

_____

_____

_____

_____

_____

_____

_____

Write down a time during your week that you can set aside for doing these activities. You may choose to do an activity during your Rest and Relaxation Day.

_____

_____

_____

_____

_____

_____

_____

_____

_____

_____

_____

_____

_____

_____

_____

_____

USE YOUR HANDS
Activity 2: Processing your Creativity

As you explore the idea of using your hands, keep a journal.

Take pictures or a video of your progress, which you can share in person or on social media.

Use the following questions to spark your journaling about your creative project.

I did these activities today:

_____

_____

_____

_____

_____

I felt

_____

_____

_____

_____

_____

I learned that

_____

_____

_____

_____

_____

I am looking forward to the following during the next creative session:

_____

_____

_____

_____

_____

I could do better by:

_____

_____

_____

_____

_____

I am pleased with myself because:

_____

_____

_____

_____

_____

ABCDEFGHIJKLMNOPQRSTU**V**WXYZ

VOLUNTEER

VOLUNTEERING IS BENEFICIAL to everyone. Besides doing something for others, you'll be doing a lot for yourself.

When you find something you care about, the act of reaching out to help is an act of personal growth. As you mature, you need other people. Infants only think about themselves until the day they connect to another person, and then their families (see "Connecting Circles of Relationships" section). Ideally, growth continues until the person becomes an active part of a community.

Volunteering is gratifying. You join with other people with whom you share a common goal. You feel good after giving of yourself and you learn new skills as a volunteer. Even a few hours a week can make a difference.

Volunteering is part of doing good things for the world. Volunteering gives us new perspectives about the world and helps us to appreciate how others live. We can look in the mirror and be grateful for what we have.

Giving to charity is often thought of only in monetary terms, but giving of your time is a substantial donation. Time is a precious commodity, so how you use your time is important. Your time is valuable.

There's a story of a distraught woman who went to her clergy and said, "I am so depressed since the injury of my son. I don't know what to do with myself." The clergy replied, "Try not to despair. If you can bring me a cup of soup from a house that has never had troubles or tragedies, I can heal your son!" The woman jumped up and exclaimed, "I will do it!" A year went by until the clergy met her on the street and asked, "What happened? You did not come back to see me." "Oh, I left your office and immediately went to the first house I saw and told them of my plight. They sat me down and told me of their problems. I offered to help them and it was good. I volunteered to take care of the cooking once a week. Then I went to the next house and explained my predicament. They also told me of great tragedy. So, I helped them. I have been so busy and now I understand that I am not the only one with disappointments and problems in life."

Volunteering may increase the endorphins flowing through the brain. Endorphins are hormones in the brain that do many positive things, such as controlling pain and feelings of stress and frustration. We feel "good" when the endorphins are flowing. The social contact and mental challenge is constructive.

Volunteering directly helps you as much or more than it helps others. Here are some benefits:

1. Feeling needed and important.

2. Feeling satisfaction at getting things done and helping others.

3. Meeting new people; gaining new friends.

4. Using your mind and body.

5. Being creative.

6. Getting active and healthier.

7. Relieving stress.

8. Getting out of your surroundings and doing something new.

9. Feeling like you are part of a community.

10. Exploring your interests.

11. Spending time doing what you care about.

12. Building confidence and self-esteem.

13. Gaining new skills.

14. Being challenged mentally and physically.

15. Discovering your talents.

If you are not volunteering, try to find some time to do so. It's a win-win for everyone.

VOLUNTEER
Activity 1: Find a Place to Volunteer

Think about what you like to do or what you personally care about. Is it animals, children, nature or the elderly? All cities and towns have opportunities to volunteer. You can volunteer in your faith community, school (even if you do not have children), library, hospitals, or animal shelters.

It is important that you not only find a place that you care about, but that you will be able to deal with emotionally.

Here are some ideas for volunteer activities in which you may wish to participate:

- Bring food to hungry people

- Find homes or clothes for those who need them

- Make neighborhoods safer and more beautiful

- Protect wildlife and natural areas

- Bring comfort and happiness to lonely people

- Care for people who are sick

- Help find cures for diseases

- Help people do better in school

- Help people to read

- Give somebody a feeling of being cared for and of hope for the future

Ask yourself these two questions:

1. Which activities of volunteering appeal to you?
   Choose three and list them in order of preference.

   _____

   _____

   _____

2. What places will offer the opportunity to you for participation in these volunteer activities? or example, the local school, Boys and Girls clubs, the local hospice, the Make a Wish Foundation....

VOLUNTEER

Activity 2: Processing the Rewards of Giving to Others

Keep a journal of your volunteering experience. Use the questions below as prompts.

I did these volunteer activities today:

_____

_____

_____

_____

I felt

_____

_____

_____

I learned that

_____

_____

_____

_____

_____

I helped by

_____

_____

_____

_____

I am looking forward to the following during the next volunteering session:

_____

_____

_____

_____

_____

I could do better by doing

_____

_____

_____

_____

_____

I am pleased with myself because

_____

_____

_____

_____

_____

WORRY NO MORE
(Anxiety)

WORRY AND ANXIETY are part of life. However, when worry and anxiety get in the way of functioning well, it is a problem. Therefore, it is how we handle the everyday stresses that are important to living a contented life. It is about our attitude.

Worry is useful for things and events that can be controlled. Worry aids in finding a solution. Once a solution is found and a decision is reached, further worry is useless and potentially harmful.

Chronic worrying is a waste of time and energy. Worrying places strain on the body. It has been pointed out that worrying about a situation in fact puts us through it twice — once when we worry about it and again when it actually happens. And if it doesn't happen, we need not have "experienced" it at all.

Anxiety and worry cause many conditions in your body. Anxiety and worry cause stress. Stress sends signals to your body to prepare for danger that is known as the "alarm reaction" for the flight or fight response. Rapid heart rate and increased breathing make sure enough blood and oxygen circulate to your major muscle groups and essential organs so you can run or fight. Nausea and stomach upset

211

result as the body shuts down systems not needed for survival, thus giving more energy to defend or flee. A dizzy or lightheaded feeling may be experienced. Also, back, neck and leg pain may result from tight, stressed muscles.

Chemicals run through our bodies to aid us during stress and result in the "flight or fight" response. But if we are constantly anxious, worried or stressed these chemicals in our bodies may be harmful.

Why may these chemicals be so harmful to us? Think of a car running all the time in fourth gear. Although the autonomic nervous system is always functioning, it uses all the gears to stay in balance. When the body is in a constant state of worry and stress, the autonomic nervous system accelerates and starts releasing the chemicals that contract your gut, increase your heart rate, elevate your blood pressure, cause sweat glands to secrete, and eventually cause failure for the organs involved. Eventually the engine is going to burn up.

Worry affects the ability to think straight. When the "flight and fight response" redirects blood and oxygen away from the brain and towards our major muscles to help them run or fight, our brains don't function properly. That's why we can't find the right words to say, or make "stupid" mistakes on tests when we are stressed.

Modern Western medicine is just now investigating the caustic effects of stress on our bodies. The Eastern art of medicine and even the ancient Greeks knew about the benefits of meditation and prayer in offsetting the negative effects of worry and stress.

When we worry to the point that it affects our everyday functioning, we are out of balance. We cannot maintain equilibrium with constant anxiety.

George was a person who worried about everything, from paying the rent, to whether or not his car would break down, to global warming. When he got into conversations, he was negative and depressing. George had trouble sleeping and bit his nails. He had not seen his father, Ben for many years. One day, he found out that his dad was gravely sick. George went to visit his father. While driving, he remembered why he did not want to be around his father. Ben was always edgy and negative. He would always criticize and worry about everything. George looked in the mirror and saw himself. He had become his father, with all the traits and behaviors that he did not like. George decided to change his life and stop worrying constantly. It was a daily and conscious effort. At first, it was hard but with practice, George did better. He realized that it is important to enjoy most of the day. George was much more content with a positive attitude.

When we stress too much, our minds and bodies are out of balance. We do not function well.

How can you tell if you worry too much?

- You fall asleep and then wake up in the middle of the night and have trouble going back to sleep.

- You are trying to do something or someone is speaking to you but you mostly focus on your worries.

- You feel and say dominantly negative comments and thoughts.

- You hands tend to be cold and at times your body is cold.

- You tend to drink or use recreational drugs to help you feel better and relax

- You can't distract yourself from your worries without them coming back and haunting you.

- You tend to get headaches.

- You tend to eat food as a comfort.

- You tend to take out your frustration on somebody else.

WORRY NO MORE
Activity 1: Stop/Reduce Worrying Techniques

To counteract worry and stress, try these techniques and find the ones that work for you.

1. Accept uncertainty. The inability to deal with uncertainty plays a huge role in anxiety and worry. Chronic worriers cannot deal well with unpredictability and doubt. Some people need to know exactly what is going to happen. Worrying is a way of predicting the future. But it does not work! Thinking about all the things that could go wrong doesn't make life any more predictable. You may feel more secure while worrying. But it is only an illusion.

2. Create a "worry time." Pick a time in the day that you can set aside for worrying (for example, 5 p.m. to 5:20 p.m.). Do not choose a time that is too close to bedtime. When you start worrying about something, write it down and then think about it during your worry time.

3. Observe yourself and catch your worrying early. Know yourself. Learn what your triggers are. When you start accelerating,

stop yourself. Once you have reached a certain level of anxiety, it is harder and harder to turn it around.

4. Slow breathing. It is valuable to do breathing exercises when you start to feel stressed. Physiologically, your body cannot go into extreme flight or fight mode when you are breathing slowly and deeply. Try it. Take a deep breath counting to six. Hold your breath while counting to six and then blow out the air while counting to six. Do this three times when feeling anxious.

5. Relaxation methods. Try to use imagery and think about something else that is not stressful. Imagine you are in your favorite place.

6. Exercise. If you can get your body moving in a positive way, it will help reduce stress. Stretching can help as well.

7. Reduce alcohol and nicotine. Nicotine is a stimulant. Stop smoking.

8. Reduce caffeine. Coffee, soft drinks and tea can make you anxious. Limit your intake of caffeine.

9. Sleep. Make sure that you are getting at least eight hours of sleep a night. (See section on *Sleep*). If your brain is not adequately rested you will be agitated and nervous.

10. Make a "to-do list" every day. Keep a pad for this purpose. Once you can see what you have to do, it is less overwhelming. Prioritize what you need to accomplish. I get pleasure from crossing completed items off the list.

WORRY NO MORE

Activity 2: Getting to Know Your Triggers (Part 1)

You need to know yourself and what triggers your anxiety and worry.

What situations cause you to worry?

Write down what happens to you physically. For example, you may get butterflies in your stomach, you may sweat more, or you may stutter.

By recognizing physical symptoms you may be able to stop this process before it gets out of control.

_____

_____

_____

_____

_____

_____

_____

So, now that you know what gives you anxiety and how that feels to you: You may try some anxiety/worry reduction techniques as discussed in Activity 1, that may stop you from worrying unnecessarily. Write down what technique you tried and the results. Do these when you start to feel anxious.

1. _____

2. _____

3. _____

4. _____

5. _____

6. _____

7. _____

8. _____

eXercise

YOUR BODY WAS CREATED to move. Exercise is a necessity as it keeps muscles toned and joints limber.

"That which is not used, slowly wears away." — Aristotle

I think that the word "exercise" has a negative connotation. For me, I associate exercise with Physical Education class where I suffered through activities that were hard and humiliating. Maybe you've tried an exercise program and failed. However, exercise should be part of your daily life, so don't give up! Let's get moving.

While exercise may be viewed as some unpleasant, hard "workout" at a gym or with an exercise tape, luckily, pleasant entertainment such as walks in nature, gardening in the yard, or building things can all provide exercise. The key is to find what you enjoy — and then enjoy it on a regular basis. Make it a pleasant hobby — not one more dreaded "To Do."

Exercise is important for many reasons.

There are physical benefits, of course. Exercise strengthens and tones muscles and bones. Studies have shown that weight-bearing movement can decrease or reverse osteoporosis. Exercise also increases flexibility, which among other things will diminish the chance for injury. As we grow older, the benefits of exercise increase. Yoga, for example, will greatly enhance flexibility and endurance.

An important part of a weight control plan, regular exercise makes us health-conscious and evidence suggests it increases our metabolism. But be careful: losing weight is more about the calories you take in than trying to burn them all away.

Beyond the physical, exercise actually reduces stress levels. So many of us today spend far too much time "in our head" and not enough out in the physical world. Exercise helps counter this and has a way of making us feel better.

Exercise also releases endomorphones in the brain — chemicals that help us to feel good. It literally improves our mood and may help decrease depression.

Exercise also helps prevent disease. It strengthens the heart muscle, which in turn helps ward off heart disease. Studies suggest exercise reduces the risk of cancer, high blood pressure, diabetes and other ailments.

Exercise is a good way to keep your physical side going and also helps the cognitive and emotional aspects by keeping your body healthy.

Shari had a back that constantly ached. She woke up sore and would take some pain relievers. Shari went to a doctor who recommended surgery. She was reluctant to have this done and went for a second opinion. The second doctor told her to get some exercises from a physical therapist. Shari was not convinced, but decided it was preferable to surgery and thus worth a try. She went to the physical therapist and learned stretching and strengthening exercises. She was amazed. Within a week, she was feeling better. She continued to do her exercises at home and improved greatly. Shari did realize that exercising needed to be a lifetime commitment.

Our bodies were meant to move. Everyone needs to exercise.

EXERCISE
Activity 1: Rethinking Exercise

The goal is to move. Get off the couch and think about the activities that you might be willing to do. Use the following list for inspiration. Then, write down the activities that you chose.

Examples:

- Vacuuming the house

- Planting flowers

- Walking the dog

- Parking away from your destination

- Walking up stairs

- Bicycling

_____

_____

_____

_____

_____

_____

_____

_____

_____

_____

Add "stretching" to the list since this is not hard for any of us.

Now, think about the above list in regards to doing activity for twenty minutes a day.

How much time per day do you spend eating? What if you could spend as much time exercising as you do eating?

Twenty minutes a day is only about two percent of your waking hours (assuming you sleep eight hours a night). Considering the benefits of physical activity, it is worth it!

EXERCISE

Activity 1: Staying Motivated to Exercise

1. Exercise is time for you. This is your time.

2. Have fun. Exercising should be fun. If it is not, then try some other activity.

3. Take note of how good you feel.

4. Take a picture of yourself at the start of the program and as you progress.

5. Give yourself rewards for exercising every week.

6. Read success stories or watch YouTube videos about success stories.

7. Find motivating quotes and post them on your computer.

8. Exercise reduces stress.

9. You may be able to fit into new clothes that are even more stylish. Go buy some new things after you have exercised for a few months.

10. Sign up for an exercise that is fun to do in a group.

11. Write an exercise log or draw a graph. It helps to have a visual about how hard (or not) you're working.

12. Exercise time is also a time that is available for thinking.

13. Exercising definitely makes you feel more attractive.

14. Read blogs of other people who have been exercising. It can help you to see that you are not alone.

15. Reaching a goal that you have set for yourself regarding your weight or clothing size. Setting a goal and tracking your progress towards it helps you to achieve it.

A B C D E F G H I J K L M N O P Q R S T U V W X **Y** Z

YOU ARE IN CONTROL

YOU CONTROL ALL your emotional reactions to life.

However, rarely do we speak in those terms. Instead, we typically use these expressions: "You made me mad," or "She makes me happy." We too often may give our power to others. But the simple truth is: You choose how you react to situations and other people. Nobody "makes" you happy or mad. You allow yourself those emotions.

Where do emotions come from? There are many theories.

One theory is that we see something and our bodies physically react. People may experience an increased heart rate, sweating, or a knot in the pit of the stomach. It's our experience —coupled with the way we perceive something — that causes us to interpret our emotion.

Take the situation of two people seeing a crowd in the park. They both may have increased alert and excitement. But one may interpret her physical response as a positive to the situation and want to join the party. Another may feel anxious about the mass of strangers and may want to get out of that area as soon as possible.

Another example of how different people react to the same thing is a motorcycle ride. One person may find riding a motorcycle exhilarating and fun, while another may find it frightening and something to avoid.

Encountering a dog walking down the street by himself is another example. One person may want to pet it and find its home, while another may be scared and run away. Perhaps the frightened individual has had bad experiences with dogs, while the other has had mostly pleasant experiences.

If you control your feelings, you are in control of your life.

Your life is full of choices.

In other words, many different viewpoints —and therefore emotions and actions —can be perceived from the same situation.

The key is realizing that you choose how you react to circumstances, even circumstances beyond your control. You can stew in helpless fury, or decide to lean back and revel in your favorite song.

Another powerful example of the mind determining feelings is with concentration camp or prisoner of war victims. Those that had an attitude of "I will make the most of this and survive to tell others" had the chance of doing so. Elie Wiesel, Victor Frankel, Heddy Spitz, Helen Handler and many others are Holocaust survivors. These people took a horrifying experience and made their lives better — not bitter.

Many people that have suffered have reached out to others. Alcoholics Anonymous and Narcotics Anonymous are two organizations that encourage people to tell their stories in the hope of helping others. These people have truly taken a lemon and made lemonade.

At one time or another, everyone gets disappointed or angry at other people. This is all about expectation. If you expect something and don't get it, you're disappointed. Maybe you expect a present from somebody that came to visit and they did not bring anything. Your reaction may be to decide they are cheap or inconsiderate. But if you had not expected something, you would not have been disappointed. You would not have felt negative feelings. Remember nobody makes you angry or happy. You make yourself angry or happy! You are in control.

Being bitter, angry, or disappointed for any reason is your choice. These negative feelings hurt you — not the person or situation you perceive caused it. And you can control your perspective and feelings. You can decide to feel and act differently. You have the power to choose better.

The same is true in reverse, by the way. No one else can make you feel happy.

The fairy tale of finding that one person to make you happy, to live "happily ever after," can do more harm than good. This idea can lead you to seek someone outside of you to fulfill your needs, when the solution can and must lie within. And in fact this very belief can chase others away. Somehow they can sense that "needy" feeling from you.

Paul believed that other people made him happy. He would go to bars and parties where everyone seemed joyous. But he often left feeling very empty. He decided to "find himself." He traveled to other countries but felt lonely and depressed. One day as he was in Cambodia, he heard children playing. He went over to see them playing soccer with a can as a ball. He saw that by many standards, these children should be miserable but they were laughing and having a great time. He joined them. He realized that it was not seeking and searching outside that he needed. His feelings came from within. He began to see that it was himself that made him happy or sad. He gained control of his feelings and his life.

Find inner contentment first. Seek that happiness within. And then see how many others are drawn to you.

You can control your emotions.

Nobody makes you feel sad or angry or happy. Take ownership of your feelings, and free yourself.

You have the power in you!

How do you know if there is greater freedom to be gained by controlling your emotions?

1. You find yourself regretting things you said.

2. You find yourself regretting things you did.

3. You are surrounded by people that bring you down or have you feeling bad about yourself.

4. You seem to do most things out of an impulse.

5. You do things and are not sure why you are doing them.

6. Friends or family members do not want to spend time with you.

If you agreed to 2 or more of these or one issue constantly, then you need to work on your emotions.

YOU ARE IN CONTROL
Activity 1: Making an Emotion Log

The first step to controlling anything is to identify it.

What are the basic emotions? They are: joy, trust, fear, surprise, sadness, disgust, anger and anticipation. Combinations of these emotions form other emotions — very much like a color wheel. For example, love = joy + trust. Disappointment = surprise + sadness.

We must be consciously aware of our emotions in order to control them.

Throughout the day, describe the situation at that moment and ask yourself how you are feeling. Do this every hour if possible. Keep a card or journal of your feelings at the moment. Beside each entry, write down what was going on around you and what was going on inside your mind. In other words, stop and analyze what you were thinking about so you can identify that emotion.

YOU ARE IN CONTROL
Activity 2

Now examine the Emotion Log you created in Activity 1.

Think about each specific situation. If you had a positive feeling, acknowledge it. Could you have felt better?

If your feeling was negative, let's evaluate this emotion. Evaluate the situation by taking a step back and thinking outside of your viewpoint. Try to look at a situation from another perspective. This will help you in several ways.

1. You become more skilled at evaluating situations objectively.

2. Taking a step back will train you to be more adept at deciding the best way to view, feel and act on a situation.

3. You are no longer just reacting to things; you are making choices.

4. You are in control of your feelings and actions. You are in control of your life.

Example:

> *1pm I was angry and insulted. My coworker brought me a piece of cake. She should have known I was on a diet. It was very inconsiderate of her.*

Different response to the same situation:

1pm My co-worker brought me a piece of cake.

New: I felt pleased that she thought about me and took the time to bring me a piece of cake. She may not have known about my diet.

ZEAL FOR LIFE AND MANAGE YOUR TIME

SAVOR THE JOY of living. Manage your time and take control. Life is a process. You can choose how your life is going to be lived. You have free will, meaning that you can choose your attitude, your beliefs and your life.

You can choose to make the most of each day.

Know that change takes time. So often we expect instant change, and grow disappointed when it doesn't happen. Remember: you did not walk before you could crawl. Be patient with yourself, and enjoy the process of learning and becoming. Be confident that change can happen. If you keep aiming for your goal, you will always be heading in the right direction.

Live every day with zeal. And watch yourself open up and bloom.

ZEAL FOR LIFE AND MANAGE YOUR TIME

Activity 1

Keep a log for a week with 15 minute intervals

- Take note of how you spend your time

- Evaluate your time as if the time was productive or at least enjoyable.

Keep in mind that we don't live by clock time. We live in real time which is in ourselves.

ZEAL FOR LIFE AND MANAGE YOUR TIME
Activity 2

Start each day with a "To Do List"

Day one

1. Make a "To Do List"
2. Prioritize the items
3. Take items to do with you when you have down time like waiting
4. Don't be afraid to say "no"
   This includes,
   Putting a Do Not Disturb sign at your desk
   Not answering the phone just because it is ringing
   Not answering every text as it comes in
   Having Facebook, Instagram or emails in front of you constantly
5. Find your most productive time. Are you a morning or evening person?
6. Try not to get sidetracked or distracted
7. Make time for relaxing and breaks. You will actually be more productive.

Day two

1. Look at the list from yesterday
2. Are there items that did not need to get done?
3. Are there times that can be delegated to others, including other's in your household?
4. What can you do better today?
5. Make a "To Do List", starting with the items that were not completed yesterday

Get some relax and get some sleep

Start process over.

About the Author

D R. LIVIA SPITZ STEINGART believes that life is what you make it. She has been working hard professionally and personally to create a better world.

Dr. Livia Spitz Steingart has five college degrees. She has a Doctorate Degree in Clinical Psychology and a Master's Degree in Psychology. Dr. Livia earned a Master's in Business Administration as a finance major. She also earned in four years, a Bachelor's Degree in Education and a Bachelor's Degree in Liberal Arts from Arizona State University graduating Cum Laude.

Her work experience includes consulting and managing medical practices, management in the corporate world, working in both, wholesale and retail businesses, teaching High School English and tutoring college students. Also, Dr. Livia was a counselor in behavioral health dealing with the severe mentally ill to people with anxiety and depression.

Dr. Livia Spitz Steingart has been happily married for more than thirty-five years and reared three children all while going to school and working.

Dr. Livia is the daughter of survivor's of the Nazi persecution. Many were murdered and the family's businesses taken away. Her parents immigrated to the United States and started over. She learned many lessons through her parents' example of working hard, learning, and caring about others in order to earn a satisfying life. Dr. Livia realized that a person can take control of one's life and make it better despite difficult situations.

Dr. Livia believes that life is a process with many ups and downs. There is no magic formula for happiness. Rather, happiness or satisfaction is something each of us may gain by being in control of ourselves and doing positive activities in the process of life.

Her book, *Life from A to Z 20 Minutes a Day: A Guide to Creating a Better You,* is about this daily process She is a remarkable individual and has accomplished much. This is her first book, devoting herself to helping make others become more of themselves.

With her book, you will be successful by just giving 20 minutes a day to yourself.

Made in the USA
San Bernardino, CA
10 June 2015